I0693659

Hamid Barole Abdu

# GENOCIDE IN RWANDA

## *Testimonies of survivors*

**ìdda**

Cover by Mouftakir Mohamed
@ 2017- 17 Hamid Barole Abdu
www.hamidbarole.it
FACEBOOK
www.facebook.com/baroleabdu
E-Mail
hamidbarole@libero.it
Mobile
Uganda:        +256.783.265.136
Italy:         +39 339.5919387



First Edition - Month November 2017-17

Printed by: idda

I dedicate this book to Anna, in the last ten years she has been with me in troubled moments, sustaining me with her wisdom, patience and affection, without losing strength despite everything.

## AUTHOR'S NOTE

When the genocide in Rwanda took place between April and July 1994, it highlighted the extent to which the Tutsi people suffered at the hands of tribalism extremists. It was especially women and children who bore the brunt of the ethnic violence that consumed Rwanda. Young girls became the spoils of the genocide. A majority of them were brutally raped, many dying as a result. The few who survived physical abuse were forced into early marriages with the men who were meting out vicious attacks on the young women and their ethnic group. Many of the girls contracted HIV/AIDS and were abandoned with children and the unborn. Although the girls were coerced into marriage, some entered into matrimony willingly, clinging on to the hope that their lives would be spared. Sadly they ended up being killed by their Hutu husbands.

Many of the females were abducted and taken to camps, where suicide was common due to the severity of the inmates' anguish. Mothers and daughters were forced to earn the right to live by selling their bodies so that their abductors could make a living. Some were even coerced into killing, and because of that many mothers slaughtered their own children either willingly or at gunpoint.

The mass slaughter of Tutsi families left many children orphaned, homeless and in some cases with no surviving kin. A large number of these resilient youngsters were traumatized by the bloody scenes they had witnessed when their parents and loved ones were killed. The hundred days of genocide were catastrophic for them; it was as though hope had turned its back on Rwanda. Many of those who had managed to escape the *Interahamwe* died of hunger and infections from either the wounds they had sustained, or from the contaminated water and food they fed on. The swamps became their homes. Some lived amongst rotting corpses while a few lucky ones managed to make their way to refugee camps in Uganda,

Congo, Tanzania and other neighbouring countries. These children ran to hospitals and churches seeking refuge, but many of them died after they were handed over to the militias by the people who were supposed to protect them. The assertion that the 1994 Rwandan genocide had no reverence and value for the young generation is far from false.

Human life was degraded beyond measure; a Tutsi's life was compared to that of a cockroach. It was absolutely meaningless and not worth living. Tutsi women and girls were reduced to sex objects who were considered unfit for marriage.

There are elements of the genocide that amplified the horrors the Hutu had visited upon the Tutsi's. One of these factors was that almost the entire population of Hutu men and women participated in callous attempts of ethnic cleansing. Hutus of all ages and classes: politicians, regional leaders, teachers, doctors, nurses, shopkeepers and taxi drivers, mothers and fathers, husbands and wives, all turned into executioners. *"The witch hunt"* against the Tutsi population had involved almost the entire population of ethnic Hutus.

Another harrowing fact is how the massacres were carried out. All kinds of objects and materials were turned into crude weapons for killing the Tutsi population: clubs or pieces of wood with nails hammered on them, machetes to open the bellies of pregnant mothers, hammers and rocks to smash their heads, holes in the ground for burying people alive. Infants and toddlers were violently thrown against walls to crush their fragile skulls; petrol was used to burn them, machetes to cut off heads or the upper and lower parts of the body and hands, feet, ears, noses.

Sanctuaries like churches, schools, hospitals became ideal settings for the massacres that had become a daily reality. The tragic paradox is that those who had the onus to protect Tutsi people in their desperate search for safety became direct or indirect assassins.

As evidence of the bloody genocide against ethnic Tutsis emerged, questions arose regarding the motive behind the majority group's actions. The Hutu ethnic group took about one million Tutsi lives over a period of about one hundred days.

Currently, many of the perpetrators are free men living in the neighboring countries, especially Congo. They are not apologetic and seem to be convinced that they did right. On the other hand, the victims of the genocide turmoil are not satisfied with the perpetrators' freedom. They had hoped for more severe punishments.

All in all, some questions still linger about with no definite answers; have the Hutus and Tutsis really reconciled? Will they ever resolve their differences amicably? Can the law help? But one thing remains for sure: both tribes need to find a way of living in harmony despite the occurrences of the past as the country continues to register social, political and economic growth.

**TITLES**

Road block killings

Manzi Escape

Mukarusine survives after numerous Militia rapes

Mukamana tells Karushara's story

Umutoni'life after Genocide

Uwamulinzi Survives the genocide

Emerine

Valentina's Narrow Death Experience

Umunyana's Tale

Assumpta's Fateful Story

Sheem's Road To Survival

Innocent Ndatimana's Narrow Escape

Valentina 2 fled to the church

Jason Nshimye

# Road block killings

Fegal lived in Rwagitima village and was 17 years old when the genocide started.

The Hutu believed that they were about to be returned to the dark ages of Tutsi autocracy. All the stories of oppression and humiliation that had been handed down from their parents, all conspiracy theories of the government and all the fear caused by the RPF incursions since 1990 had been whipped up by extremist politicians to produce a pathological hatred towards the Tutsi.

President Habyarimana's plane crash took place on April 6 and some local Hutus immediately planned their retaliation while others eagerly waited for what would happen next. A few Tutsis left the country then, anticipating disorder. But nothing could have prepared them for what was about to happen.

Fegal was traveling to the next village to visit a friend when their taxi found a roadblock. There were Hutus with machetes raised up as they sang loudly. Many taxis and personal vehicles had been stopped and Tutsis were being asked to step out. Those who hesitated were forcefully pulled out of the cars and tortured. Fegal recalls a woman whose hair was pulled through the window since she had refused to move out and the man chopped her head off. It fell outside and the body remained inside. Everyone looked on helplessly.

Fegal only remembers the face of one man. He had wild matted hair, his eyes were red, he came and asked them to present their identity cards and Fegal's stomach was churning fear because he thought they might take him since he was mixed blood of the Tutsi and the Hutu. He presented it to the man and he was asked to join the safe group while the rest were singled out, beaten and humiliated.

When they were approaching the main road to reach us, they were shot dead by the very men who had raped them. We were spared because the men in charge of the killings were tribe mates to some two men. Those two men from the spared group moved to the bodies crying, they were their wives. They asked why they killed them. The man went to them and said to them that their wives deserved to die because they have no right to live, he asked the men to get the machete and take off their heads. They were both crying and one of them said that he couldn't do it to his wife; the *Interahamwe* militia raised his machete and chopped the man's hand apart. He cried loudly while bleeding heavily next to his wife's body. They asked the second one to finish his wife too or else he would have the fate of his friend. He raised the machete and cut off the wife's head for fear of being killed.

"*The Militia asked us to join them to finish all the Tutsi in the country which some men in my group accepted and were given the weapons and asked to kill any Tutsi around them.*" Fegal and others were asked to carry the bodies to tracks.

When Fegal and others went to throw the bodies in the swamp, they found a team of Tutsis who were hidin. They asked them not to tell the others because they were going to kill them if they knew that they were still alive. They were hiding in a small team supporting one another. The swamp was strewn with dozens of dead bodies. Some of the people who were using it as a hiding place died of fever and diarrhea. Fegal and others asked them to go far inside the swamp because others were to come to dump more bodies and they would see them.

Evening came and Fegal couldn't continue his journey because he was then under the militia orders. They moved to another road spot since that was known and few Tutsis could pass there to escape.

Militia asked them to get beers from shops around and they found it easy since many had already left their shops in fear for their lives. They drunk almost the whole night but by morning the killers were sober ready to start the killings. When it got to the evening, they drank beers like water as a way of rewarding their work. They continued to kill and used the young to steal for them. On the other side it was an advantage to the Tutsis because the more the militia drank in the night, the more their schedule to kill others the next day was delayed. It helped the Tutsis to escape especially during the early hours of the morning.

The militia soon realized that fewer people were using the roads. So they asked Fegal's group to pass the message that it was from the municipal judge to go door to door killing the Tutsi without the exception of age. He remembers some boys asking if they were to take possession of some properties that belonged to the Tutsi after killing them. The answer was *"There is no need to ask how to begin, but immediately to start from the bush, and now."* They gave them machetes to finish the Tutsis.

That same day, some came to the meeting without a machete or other cutting tool. The *Intarahamwe* lectured them and said it would pass once but should not happen twice, they told them to arm themselves with tree branches and stones and form barriers at the rear to stop any Tutsi escaping. They showed them leaders to follow and nobody ever forgot his machete again.

Keep going until the end, maintain a satisfactory pace, spare no one and loot everything found. The first rule was to kill and there was no second rule. It was an organization with no complications. They went on to gather the Tutsis and killing them. The only directive was to kill all.

They were also the commands which were called the Hutu Ten Commandments. They stated that:

1. All Hutus must know that the Tutsi woman wherever she may be is serving the Tutsi ethnic group and in consequence any Hutu who does the following was taken to be a traitor: To have a Tutsi wife, Tutsi mistress and anyone who acquires a Tutsi dependant.

2. All the Hutu had to know that the Hutu daughters are worthy and more conscientious in their role of woman, spouse and mother. No other women were more beautiful, better secretaries and more sincere than the Hutu.

3. Hutu women, be vigilant and bid their husbands, brothers and sons to come to their senses.

4. All Hutus had to know that the Tutsi were dishonest in business that their only goal was ethnic superiority.

5. The strategic political, administrative, economical, military and security positions had to be reserved for Hutus.

6. The education sector (students, teachers) had to be Hutu majority.

7. The Rwandan armed forces had to be exclusively Hutu because the 1990 war taught them a lesson as no military man was to marry a Tutsi woman.

8. Hutu had to stop taking pity on Tutsi people.

9. They had to be united from wherever they were. They had to be strong and vigilant to their Tutsi enemy.

10. The social revolution of 1959, the 1961 referendum and the Hutu ideology had to be taught to all Hutu at all levels.

All the Hutu had to widely spread the message. Any Hutu who persecuted his Hutu brother for having read, spread and taught the above ideology was a traitor.

The killing season was on and Fegal with others rose up earlier than the usual to eat lots of meat and they went up to the soccer field at around ten o'clock and their leaders would grumble those who came late and then left to attack. They set Tutsi houses on fire, destructed all the properties that they got around.

Fegal says: *"Killing was very discouraging even if you decided to do it even to an animal but we had to obey the orders of the authorities. If you had not been well prepared, you felt yourself pushed and pulled, and if you thought that the killing did not have disastrous consequences for yourself, you felt soothed and reassured then you went off with no more worries."*

In the afternoon they didn't sing because they were tired but they left for their homes while Fegal and others went back to fields were they gathered. They fortified themselves with beers and the meat from the animals they had slaughtered and then returned to the killings. Fegal was now a real militia having used his machete many times. He spotted a group of the Tutsis trying to escape, creeping through the mud like snakes. Fegal and the other militia ran through the mud and slashed off their heads while others forcefully dropped the Tutsis' heads into the mud, killing them. For some killers, such insults were just minor diversions but the important thing was not to let the Tutsi escape alive while to other killers the taunts were revitalizing and made those killings easier to do.

In night after the killings, Fegal and others scattered out to dig in the fields to collect beans and bananas that they would prepare before the next day.

*"Had the RPF delayed one more week, they would have found no surviving Tutsi in the region,"* says Fegal.

Shortly after, the RPF soldiers reached Kayonza. Government soldiers ran away in one direction while Fegal with the other *Intarahamwe* took off in the other way. The soldiers started fleeing while asking the civilians to return home but they felt it still dangerous since some of the killers had mixed with civilians. Fegal was one of those who went towards Kayonza which meant that he was mixed with the innocent Tutsi. He was scared that people would identify him and give him to the RPF but he had no option. The place was crowded; some of them went and occupied Mukarange empty houses.

Six days later, people who had seen Fegal and others killing people pointed them out to the RPF soldiers but he was the only one from his commune. The rest came from Muhazi and Kabarondo. Fegal was taken to prison with other Hutu who had engaged in the killings.

While in prison Fegal was visited by persons whose relatives he had killed to reveal to them where he and the group had left their remains. Through Gacaca court, Fegal asked for forgiveness and was thanked for coming out and confessing. He chose to serve half of his sentence in community service known as TIG (Travaux de interest Generaux; building roads, making bricks or rebuilding houses for survivors while his other friends who didn't confess served their full sentences in prison.

Though he confessed his crimes, his conscience still accuses him of killing innocent people. *"I must prevent wrong doing in any way because I know how far it has taken me,"* he says.

Many other people without the necessary training were forced to do similar things while others killed by their will. The *bourgmstre* brought *intarahamwe* from other communes when the killings started on 9th.

*"People like Gatete should be punished or even killed for forcing people to kill their neighbors,"* Fegal states. He was scared to return to his village even after serving his punishment for fear of revenge from the victims' families.

## Manzi Escape

Manzi was 15 years in 1994, living with his two parents and the grandmother who had come to visit them for some days. Before the real genocide, people were being killed quietly. But after President Juvenal Habyarimana's death, it became open.

Manzi's father was a Seventh day Adventist pastor who had lived through the Rwandan revolt for independence from the Belgium. His mother was from a Tutsi tribe. It was early morning in Sovu village Butare District when they were still in bed but the father had got up to prepare for the church service because it was a Sunday. They started hearing gunshots, people not so far away from their house were screaming and when they looked through the window, homes were burning and many people running in different directions with their children crying.

Nzeyimana , Manzi's father told them to get up saying: *"All I can say is go find refuge, go find a place to hide but wherever you will be, keep praying that we meet again. After the end of it all we shall live together."*

Then immediately, Manzi moved out with the grandmother as father and the mother were taking some important documents. When they moved to the bush where many were heading to, grandmother stopped to see if the others were coming but they couldn't see them. They went back to the house but as they got there, Manzi saw his father taken to the road side near their home, was shot on the head while his mother was locked inside the house and it was set on fire. They were hiding in the bushes around and he was bitten by a snake. Manzi tried to get back to his grandmother but only found her lined with others near a toilet pit that was dug for toilet purpose. His grandmother and others saw him and asked him to go. They tried to show him a way to escape.

His grandmother told him: *"Go! We are going to be killed; we don't want you to die with us!"*

Manzi left the village running to the save his life. He tied the leg that had been bitten by a snake and tried to move on. On his way he met a neighbor who was well known to him and was with his family in their car heading to the Uganda boarder. Manzi joined and they moved on. The neighbor's wife was bleeding having sustained a wound from being stoned as they escaped the *intarahamwe* men who had attacked their house as well.

A few miles away from their village, they were stopped by a roadblock and were all asked to move out. When the militia saw the woman bleeding, they pulled her out of the car and figured that the family was escaping. They were all asked to kneel down, the woman was crying loudly because her two children were locked in the car. One of the militia men opened the tank cover of the car and lightened the match to set the car on fire. The mother of the children inside got up to move to the car, the same man smashed off her left leg and said that's what they do if you get up without their permission.

The husband was asked to take her away from the car that had started burning with the two children inside. As he pulled her away, the militia chopped off his hand too. They were on the ground screaming like chickens whose heads had been cut off. Manzi was now the only one still aside kneeling, just waiting for his turn. He saw one of the children in the burning car on the window trying to break out, calling her mother and father for help but they couldn't. It caught fire and made a blast that everyone including the militia had to get far from it. When it blasted, the husband got up and tried to run to a nearby bush but was shot in the back and pulled back. Manzi was then ordered to take off his head by a machete. He held the machete but before doing it, a speedy car came to the roadblock firing gun shots at the militia so as it could continue. They all went down while they tried to shoot back at it. Manzi was left with the machete in his arms and no was concentrating on him anymore so he used the chance to escape to the bush and continue to run.

In the bush, Manzi met some people who were also hiding. When they saw him with the machete they wanted to kill him thinking he was a militia man but he explained and was left. With no more sustenance other than a daily water drop, Manzi begun to find himself obsessed with food and death.

*"We closed our eyes at night and dreamed about food and our families and when I was about to eat the food with my family, I woke up. Sometimes we looked at those who were about to die and thought they were lucky to die soon or die with all their body parts together. We thought they were not to suffer any more."*

It was the same fate for adults and the children in the bush .They had no chance of food and milk for the babies and this caused many people not even stuck by machete to be sprung by a deadly weakness. Manzi woke up one morning to find the person who had slept close to him stiffened in his sleep. And whenever that happened, Manzi and the others only left that place to go hide somewhere without even covering the bodies.

On the rainy nights Manzi and the group rubbed themselves down with palm leaves cleaning away the thickest coatings of refuse and the mud filth. After they lay down on the ground, they spent the night talking of the day, asking about who had died that day and who was to follow next. They talked about the evil fate that had fallen on their heads and did not exchange words of joy rather than the despondent ones.

In the hide out Manzi and the group could not access any news because radios could no longer be listened to except in the homes of the Hutu killers. They heard from other people that the genocide had spread over the country and that all the Tutsi were suffering the same way so they believed no one would come to save them until death. This made Manzi less concerned about when he would die since they were all to die in some way but he only thought of how the cuts would hack to him and how long it would take him to die because he was very frightened of the machetes bestow.

On certain evenings, when the evildoers had not killed too much that day, Manzi would gather around with the group glowing embers to eat something cooked but other evenings they were discouraged in order to prevent easy allocation by the killers. They tried to run together in small teams to inspire courage in each other and he who was surprised in an ambush was killed and those who got tired also died.

"The bush where we were hiding smelt of human dead. Flies, birds and dogs were feeding on our dead friends, families and relatives."

Manzi went out of the bush with another man to find medicine from a Hutu friend they thought could help them. On arrival, they knocked at the back door and he opened the window to see who was at the door. Good enough they knew each other but he was not happy because this man had taken Manzi to a Hutu's house. He gave them food and asked them to leave because he would be in danger if they found out that his visitors were inside. He gave them clothes to change, little medicine and asked them to leave and not to return. On leaving, he directed them to a point where they would wait for him from the next morning to take them to a safe place. Manzi and the friend moved out but never went too far where he had asked them to wait. They slept with the cows at the back of the house and when he opened the door early the next morning, he brought his car and locked them in the boot.

With his help they managed to get to a cathedral in Kigali where 1500 people were hiding. The number of sanctuary seekers gradually diminished as Hutus arrived to take small groups out to be murdered. When they dropped them to the church, he returned home while Manzi and the friend went to the church. Men and women plus children had escaped to the church thinking that the militia couldn't come to the house of God to kill them. They shared food that was collected and cooked all together by all those in the cathedral. After three days at the cathedral, while they were sleeping with the church doors closed, the militia men came and asked those inside to open the door, threatening to bomb the church.

They opened and the men came inside grabbing women whom they had sexual interests in and those who tried to cry for their women were added to the group. If she had a baby, she would be added to the group as well. Whoever was taken never returned. They took them, raped them, killed the husbands and the babies. They always came after a little while and when they took long to open for them, they used grenades to break through the church walls.

The killers informed them that they were tired of the slow pace that they were using to kill them. and said they would be back the next day to bomb all the church down with grenades. They people were scared but couldn't leave because there was no any other safe place for them. Manzi knew that it was his turn to meet his family. He didn't sleep that night but rather tossed and turned, imagining his death.

Manzi believes it was God who gave him another chance to life. The friend with whom he had come left the church after hearing that they were going to bomb it. He was spared after he paid 20p bribe to the soldiers and escaped to the Uganda boarder.

The massacres started at about 9:00am the next morning and it continued until 5:00pm. However, at about 2pm, the hiding place where Manzi was was set on fire by petrol and he felt it, he tried to get out of the burning house and he was shot but fortunately he was not wounded. He fell down to the ground and out of the burning house, he stayed stretched but he could hear everything going on.

Towards 5:30pm seven gendarmes arrived and stopped the killings. They asked the killers to loot all that was necessary. They also asked the girls and women who were not yet dead to come and promised them protection. When Manzi heard that from the ground where he was lying, he got up. They were many in number, but on the ground survivors were still bleeding. One could barely find space to step foot. They calmed them down and moved them to the main road.

When they arrived they asked them to sit beside the road. Manzi thought death was coming to all of them but they talked among themselves and asked them to move back to the cathedral. It was already dark and the ground was still covered with dead bodies but they had to move back. That same night, Manzi left because he thought the killers would return to kill them all. He went to his aunt was a Hutu and did not stay very far from the Cathedral but she refused to open for him. He then resorted to the aunt's neighbor who he knew from the many visits he used to pay his aunt. She too didn't open. He couldn't think of anyone else he could turn to.

The genocide had turned relatives into enemies; he spent the night over the aunt's roof. The next day the aunt threatened to hand him over if he didn't leave her home. When she left, the neighbor was kind enough to hide him in her house without the husband's notice.

"After two nights under the bed she asked me to leave since the husband was getting suspicious." Manzi went back to cathedral that night and found the rebels had arrived to rescue all those inside.

Manzi doubts that it was bravery that saved him since he was too young to be courageous. *"Perhaps I could say I was able to disguise myself when I went to different areas and found a Hutu,"* he says.

After five years Manzi gathered his mother and grandmother's bones from the pit and cleaned them for burial. Life is still a struggle for him because he is an under educated worker who earns less from the odd jobs. Tears still come out his eyes every time he remembers his parents.

## Mukarusine survives after numerous Militia rapes

Mukarusine was a 19year old, fifth year secondary school student at Gitarama, Nyabisindu. She narates the conquests of women who she still thinks were the spoils of the genocide. Mukarusine was under intense pressure from her abductor's female relatives to give herself to him. Though she didn't suffer the extreme cruelty to which so many Tutsi women were subjected, Mukarusine reveals the way in which her status was reduced to chattel, even in the eyes of other women.

She is the only survivor in her immediate family. Her parents, three sisters and two of her brothers were killed in Nyanza, Gitarama on April 12, 1994. When the killings began, her family ran in different directions. Mukarusine, her two remaining brothers and the young sister of 15 went to Butare in Nyabisindu. Her brothers continued on while Mukarusine, her sister and the friend hid in a trench until they were captured on 17th. Her young sister was abducted by the leader of the local killers. Mukarusine was taken to the cliff were she witnessed people's heads being cut off and clubbed in front of her. She was protected by some neighbors from those who were determined to kill her. Mukarusine's future abductor, Marcel, a driver, then arrived and saved her from execution. She had seen this man in the neighborhood but had never spoken to him.

They went together and along the way he tried to rape her. Mukarusine cried and pleaded with him to leave her. The man seemed genuinely upset at seeing her so distraught. He told her that in future Mukarusine should regard him as a brother and took her to hide at the home of his older brother, the one who had tried to save her life before. While she was there, a Tutsi man who had been hiding in the bush came to the house. He had been so overcome by hunger that he took the risk and made the deal that he would pay him for food and in exchange to hide him.

The *intarahamwe* began to check houses. The man was hidden in the cowshed while Mukarusine went to the nearby bush and hid. They discovered the man and led him away and didn't find Mukarusine from the bush. The owner of the house told Mukarusine that they killed the Tutsi man and fined him for hiding a Tutsi. With these developments Marcel became worried about Mukarusine's security and proposed hiding her at his mother's house. When Mukarusine got there, she became terrified about the things they said were happening around every Tutsi. Some family members had witnessed some of the awful things the *intarahamwe* were doing to the Tutsi both men and women. They said that some women had been taken to the road side and forced to watch the killing of Tutsi men, after which they would be given lectures by one of the key killers, a one Karaguye. They said that he had told them *"You Tutsi women, you have no respect for Hutu men. So now choose between death and marrying the Hutu intarahamwe."* He promised them that their deaths would be crueler than the ones they just witnessed.

They went looking for the filthiest looking vagabonds and jigger infested and others. They looked for a kind of man who was least likely to get a woman under normal conditions. There were so many women that they could not find enough of those dirty men but the fear of being killed was so intense that the women would plead and ask those men to take them.

After a few days, the mother started pestering her son for leaving Mukarusine alone. She said that *"Everybody else is getting married and you have a woman, what are you keeping her for?"* Mukarusine thinks the man wanted to take her but he didn't know how to tell her. The earlier incident had clearly frightened him. So he came up with a false story about how members of <u>CDR</u> had ordered all Hutu me to kill the Tutsi women they had taken, or else run the risk of being killed themselves. He said that it was already known by the Hutu that Mukarusine was with him and said that the choice was up to her. She asked him to tell them that they were married. He dismissed the idea and blackmailed her saying that Mukarusine never liked him because he was a Hutu. He threatened her by saying *"drop your Tutsi arrogance, in case you will not find a Tutsi man afterwards as they have all been killed"*. She said it was nothing against him but she was not ready for marriage. He asked *"When will you be ready?"*, and Mukarusine she would be ready in four years. He laughed and said *"Well, right now you have a choice to make and that choice is marriage or death"*. She said she preferred death. He laughed louder saying *"You can afford to say that because you are here protected in my mother's house. You should see how your fellow Tutsi are urinating in their pants, pleading to Hutu men to take them as they are afraid of death. You don't know what kind of death you will face otherwise you wouldn't talk rubbish."*

Mukarusine pleaded with him until he finally agreed to tell the militia that they were married. They agreed to get married once the war was over. When he told people that they were married, some believed him while others didn't. His mother knew the truth and after some days, she threatened to throw Mukarusine out unless she agrees to marry her son for real.

Trying to twist her arm she said: *"Your only objection to my son is the fact he is a Hutu."* She went ahead and brought some elderly women to the house to insult her. These women accused her of being childish and one of them said: *"Women of your kind have been taken by dogs like vagabonds, and here you are rejecting this nice young man, your sister who is fourteen is already married what are you waiting for?"*

By that time she knew where her sister was, they started visiting each other at night. She said she had no choice but to sleep with her abductor. He was a real killer and had she refused, she would have been killed. Mukarusine knew that what gave her strength to resist was a confidence and instinct that she was to survive the genocide.

The old woman continued to pester his son to take her and kept saying she was the only Tutsi woman in the area living with a man without being turned into his wife. Marcel's mother and his friends who had abducted Tutsi women began to taunt Marcel saying he was impotent so he used whatever he could to get Mukarusine to marry him. He even sent his brother's wife to intercede for him. She began by pointing out the stupidity of the mess they had created and advised her to pick a leaf from her sister, a young girl who was being kept by a much older killer.

She added, *"at least you are with descent people and don't fear for your future because you will still be able to get married"*. The old woman also pointed out that she couldn't go on hiding Mukarusine without marriage to her son, saying that the other option was for Makarusine to leave them and run the risk of getting killed. But still Mukarusine refused.

One morning, the old woman went to see her with two other elder women. They criticized and threatened her and when Marcel came in, he was in a complete state and informed her that she had to leave the house and he was planning to take her to Karege, the leader of killers in the local area. It became clear to Mukarusine that he was serious this time but she said to him that she was able to take herself to the killers. Marcel insisted of taking her. She told him that she was able to leave their house as they wanted by her own and she stood up to leave. Marcel looked very worried and started following her. His mother prohibited him from bringing her back to the house unless it was for marriage. Mukarusine sent a message to her sister's abductor asking him to escort her to Karege's place. He arrived and told her to stop being so childish, he asked: *"Are you superior to all these other women?"* but she didn't answer him and requested him to take her to the house where she knew a cousin was hiding. When they got there, a member of the family hiding her cousin told her that Hutu houses suspected of hiding Tutsi were being carefully searched. Telling her that one of her brothers who Mukarusine hoped was alive had recently been killed and she was advised to be realistic.

The conversation was taking place on the street while Marcel was right behind them and after the conversation he asked her to follow him. He took her to another house belonging to a relative of his mother who was keeping Mukarusine's sister and shortly after Marcel left for his job in Butare. He promised to return for her, but in the meantime people in Nyanza got to know that Mukarusine and the sister survived by getting married.

The order was passed to hunt all Tutsi women down. It was in Nyanza where it was declared that *"If a snake wraps itself around the milk calabash, you don't let it survive for the sake of the calabash"*. When they went to Marcel's mother's house, they didn't find her there. They beat up the Hutu girl found there, trying to make her reveal where Mukarusine had gone but she didn't know. She took them to Mukarusine's little sister and tried to force the sister to say where she was hiding but also didn't and then she was killed. After the news, the man hiding her said he could not keep her any longer. She was completely distraught by the news of the sister's death; she didn't consider it worth living any more. She asked them to hand her over to the killers and later she decided to go to the killers herself and Mukarusine walked towards Karege's house.

An entrepreneur who had been building a house for her father, tried to dissuade her from giving herself up. He offered to hide her but she didn't pay any attention to him, she was sick of hiding that she didn't even want to hear the word. The entrepreneur kept following her trying to convince her that it was wrong to allow her sister's death to decide the fate of her life. But to her, her sister was all she was left with and then she was gone, she had no reason to live for. She was also reluctant to go with the entrepreneur. On their way, a certain man asked the entrepreneur about his wife's condition.

"When I heard that the entrepreneur had a wife, I knew I would be safe at his house. However, he didn't take her to his house but rather to an incomplete house he was building. A 15year old girl and her brother also came to hide in the house. They were from a Tutsi family that was known for being wanted. People had seen them coming to the house and this made Mukarusine afraid. The entrepreneur made arrangements with a young *intarahamwe* to guard her and tried to convince her that she would have no problems, whatever the danger she had no choice anyway.

Mukarusine discovered that there was a conspiracy between the two men, they tried to scare her by saying that if she went to Nyanza where her father was well know, she was to die a painful way with a lot of torture. They said that the intarahamwe at every roadblock had her name and description.

The young intarahamwe came to her with the aim of raping her. He took her to his house and didn't touch her for the first day saying that he wanted her to get used to him. He told her that he had made arrangements with the entrepreneur to have her. To make sure Mukarusine got the message; he displayed grenades and bullets and said *"make your choice".* This time Mukarusine had no choice but to submit, she explained to the man what she had gone through but nothing moved him. He kept her for five days and when she reflected on everything, the only consolation she could find was to tell herself that if she would have been raped for a much longer period.

Like other young women who had been raped and left alone in the world after the murder of everyone she knew and loved, Mukarusine saw no point in continuing her life because her torment made worse by the propaganda on radio which stated that the Rwandese army was defeating the RPF and that there was no hope for all the Tutsi. Mukarusine decided to kill herself by the grenades of her abductor but they were away, frustrating her desires to commit suicide. Mukarusine and the group of other girls and women were saved when the RPF attacked the area.

## Mukamana tells Karushara's story

In 1959 King Rudahigwa died. Thereafter massacres of Tutsi were organized. Many thousands of Tutsis were killed while others fled to neighboring states. In 1961 they held elections. The first government Prime Minister was Gregoire founder of the Parmehutu, a party for the emancipation of the Hutu. A year, Rwanda gained independence. The regime was characterized by the persecution and ethnic cleansing of Tutsis. In ethnic divisions, the Kayibanda regime created regional divisions which contributed to the d'etat by Major General Juvenal Habyarimana in 1973.

The Belgians presented Tutsi as an alien race and used physical features as a way to differentiate from the indigenous Hutu. Adding race to Rwandan identity cards in 1930s, they counted 15% as being Tutsi, 84% as Hutu and 1% as Twa. Ethnic identity began to determine Rwandan lives.

Habyarimana used the tension to exploit divisions in the population, launching campaigns of persecution and fuelling fear among the people. The war on the Tutsi minority was going largely unnoticed even though many Tutsi and Hutu opponents of the divisive ideology were in prison tortured and others murdered.

Habyarimana's MRND was responsible for establishing the Interahamwe, a flamboyant and potentially dangerous Hutu youth militia that gained enormous popularity. Advocating Hutu power and Hutu at the expense of Tutsi lives, their message was reinforced and spread by an extremist media. By 1990 the genocide ideology of Hutu power had perfected.

Mukamana was 28years and lived in the sector governed by a woman called Karushara. Karushara was fifty three and a councilor in the sector of Kimisagara in Kigali, she lived in Kimuhoza. She is originally from Bwakira in Kibuye. She used to sell beer before she was appointed in charge of Kimuhoza then appointed as councilor of Kimisagara by Fracois Karera who was her close ally. She took an extremely active role in the genocide wearing military uniform throughout. She was tall and a physically strong woman, she used to beat up the Tutsi herself before handling them over the intarahamwe men for final killings. She distributed arms to the assassin and was frequently at the roadblocks in the sector she was leading, deciding on spot who was to be killed and who to live.

She held meetings in her house in a place called Ntaraga with the intarahamwe on how to finish the Tutsi in the country. The distribution of weapons to the killers in her sector was carried out in her house and those massacred were dumped in River Nyabarongo while other bodies were dumped in the mass grave around the hides and skin factory known as SODEPARAL. Others were killed in front of her house and bodies taken away to swamps under her command. Karushara was a widow and a mother of five children, three boys and two girls. Two of her sons, Mugenzi and Mutabaruka were drivers and the third was a high school student. One of the daughters Mukaperezida was married and the other daughter Nyirandegeya was a single mother. Twenty four year old Mutabaruka was the driver during genocide and carried gun and machetes. He drove in the sector her mother was leading to ensure work was being done as her mother had instructed. The other son was a killer and murdered people who were captured and those his mother wanted.

With the progressive advance of the RPF, Karushara became wilder, she managed to hold off the gendarmes guarding her house and trained them, and they were the future militia men. They guarded *electrogaz* at the same time. It was said they could poison the water and they gave it to the Hutu to drink. With the death of

Bueyana on February 22$^{nd}$ 1994, death squads invaded the neighborhood of Kimisagara and many Tutsi left their families. In the evening, Radio Muhabura said that Karushsra had increased the killings of Tutsi in her sector. Soldiers came and set up in the neighborhood with their families saying that the military camps where saturated. But they had come to kill the Tutsi in the sector.

On 7$^{th}$ April things turned upside down in a little time, Karushara had a chance to prove her loyalty to the MRND. In the early morning of 7$^{th}$, there had already been an attack against Mukamana's house. He escaped following the Kimisagara road thinking that the UNAMIR soldiers would save him and others. They attacked his house but no one was there because Mukamana had sent his family to a place where he thought it was safe. The plan was decided at Karushara's home. Mukamana went with a lot of money to the first sergeant's house and asked him to hide him, but the sergeant said that he had no need to hide because they were looking for accomplices of the inkotanyi, meaning people that the militia men were accusing of something. He stayed at the church all day and never closed his eyes.

Karushara came with the killers to the church and killed Kabguza, a Hutu who was married to a Tutsi woman. He had followed her wife to the church for safety. He was killed with a machete by the orders of Karushara and the wife was taken out of the church and burned by petrol. She came back inside and pointed at a moderate Hutu who worked for the government and was also killed by the machete. She later carried her gun, dressed in the militia uniform and went out.

On the 10$^{th}$ the militia found him inside his house and accused him of being an RPF spy in Kigali. They led him to the roadside and asked other people. They said he was a good man who couldn't involve himself in such. Mukamana was not killed but was forced to go the roadblock like other patriotic Rwandese. He offered money and was set to go back to his home. After two days they attacked him again and the sergeant friend protected him but they went to Karushara and reported the sergeant. She summoned a meeting were she said that Mukamana was to be killed in few days. There was delay in implementing the order and on 5th May Karushara's son called Pascal came and fired on Mukamana, his arms were up as he asked for forgiveness. He was shot on the left arm and in the stomach and he fell down. He heard them telling the shooter to finish him but he was out of bullets. So he went to pick from the other militia men around at the base nearby. They both went as they thought he was at the point of death and he used the chance to get up and run fast towards Nyabugogo where he was caught on the road block. He told them he was a victim of the RPF and they took pity on him, put him in a car and went to CHK.

After two days, he decided to go Kaduha where he had a sister working as a nurse with Sister Melgitta to seek refugees. He reached Kaduha Health Centre and found many Tutsi refugees from all over the sous-prefecture of Kaduha, which encompasses commune Muko and Musange. Karambo rushed to the Parish which was made up of two primary schools and the church and they were increasing in number. Sister Melgitta was helping to provide porridge for them as they were locked in the healthy centre. But staring from the 17th, they began to prevent people from bringing food and the Tutsi could no longer leave the church freely. They were stopped by people who put up barricades. If you decided to go out, if you decided to go home and get some food, they would kill you.

It was on April 20th when the group of attackers who had come from all different areas surrounded them in one kilometer distance and the killings started at 8:00am. They threw a grenade to the teachers' house at Kaduha Agriculture and Veterinary School and later surrounded the Kaduha hospital. Only a small street separated the school and the health centre. They could easily communicate with those on the other side. At 9am, the killers came to the hospital, armed with machetes. Some of them were well known to some people because they came from the same village. They included several women and girls while others like Louise worked at Kaduha health centre as an auxiliary nurse and was from Butare. She was terrible and had a long sword that she dragged on the cement every evening to sharpen it. The noise it made alone scared everyone. They came into the hospital and forced the sick outside and killed them with a machete, they knew where to hit on the head and as soon as they had finished, they threw them on the grass near the hospital. The girls walked around to finish those who were lying on the ground. The killers didn't kill everyone because they were afraid of Sister Melgitta's centre.

As the attacks extended from one hill to the next and from one commune to another, Tutsis found it impossible to stay in their homes and increasingly difficult to hide with Hutu neighbors. Assailants in Muko, for example, were threatening to make Hutu protectors kill any Tutsi whom they had sheltered. First hundreds, then thousands of people from Musebeya, Muko, Karambo, and Musange communes gathered at Kaduha parish center, in the church itself, in the adjoining schools, in the health center and in all the spaces in between. Tutsi from more distant regions, like parts of Muko, came first. Tutsi in the immediate vicinity of the church moved there only about April 14, when they were threatened with attacks by Hutu from the hills. Many Tutsi had come on their own, but some had come with the help of local officials, like those transported from Musebeya. In Muko, and perhaps elsewhere, the burgomaster had at first refused to help Tutsi flee to Kaduha, but later changed his position and began encouraging them to go there.

Some survivors believe that authorities decided at a meeting at the sub-prefecture to attract Tutsi to Kaduha for one enormous massacre rather than to continue killing them in smaller numbers throughout the area. Such a decision would have been consistent with the pattern of killings elsewhere in the country. On April 18, the newly arrived police sergeant-major together with the sub-prefect reportedly forced Tutsi to leave the hospital and go to the church area. Sister Melgitta who ran the health center was allowed to keep only Tutsi patients who appeared seriously ill. They were taken out and killed. After several hours of shooting and throwing grenades, the assailants paused temporarily while awaiting new supplies of ammunition. During that period, they continued killing by machete, spear, club, and other weapons. Mukamana heard gunfires and the explosion of grenades and the cries of people being killed. The attackers fired their guns and threw grenades into the crowd and then groups of killers with traditional weapons came in and killed those who were still alive. This began early morning on the 21st and it continued through Thursday and Friday. On Friday, they mostly searched for people who were hiding but Mukamana pretended as the Sisters worker and was hiding in her bedroom.

After a little while, when the rebels had arrived, Mukamana left for St. Famille Church. He forced himself on z UNAMIR vehicle and moved to the church to find his family. Unfortunately his wife and six children had all not survived the genocide. They were murdered in Kimisagala. He doesn't know how but all he knows is that wherever they lie, they have more peace than he can ever achieve because pain and sorrow will never reach them like what he's going through. A group of Tutsi broke out of the encirclement and fled to the northeast to save life but they encountered military and civilian assailants waiting along the roads for them. A new radio antenna had been installed in Kaduha shortly before and it may have made it easier for the police to inform their troops about the movements of the refugees. When the military encountered the fleeing Tutsi, they ordered them to sit down and then began firing at them and throwing grenades into their midst.

# Umutoni's life after Genocide

Umutoni Jane was born in the Southern Province of Rwanda. Her parents were cattle keepers with ten children. They are now four because the other six died during the genocide. Before the genocide, Umutoni never experienced any violence. The first time she encountered violence was during the genocide, when she was nineteen years old.

Umutoni was raped and she gave birth to a child of an Intarahamwe. Umutoni has good memories of her life before the Genocide, especially meeting up with her friends. It hurts that she no longer sees them because the genocide separated them. Umutoni now lives with her three children and a husband. The oldest child is seventeen years old, the second one is three years old, and the last one is one year old.

At the beginning of the genocide they were all home. They saw houses being burned on the other side of the neighborhood. Suddenly Umotoni saw many aggressive men coming towards their home. They had machetes and sticks. She then heard her mother telling them: *"Run away because they are coming to kill us."* They fled separately, each searching for a place to hide. Umotoni decided to hide in the forest, expecting nobody to find her there. She spent three days alone in the forest. Then the Interahamwe found her with others who had hid in the bush, the boys and men were hacked with machete while others were taken to be killed on the main road. Umotoni and three other girls were spared by the militia men who had sexual interests in them. They were taken in the house of a Tutsi man who had escaped, together with the three girls and were raped.

Most of them left as soon as they arrived, but four of them stayed with her. They tore her clothes to pieces and started to rape her one after another while the others watched. After that catastrophic experience, Umotoni lost consciousness. When she woke up, she was still in the same place. After regaining some strength, she got up and wandered aimlessly in the streets. Seeing her like that all naked, the Interahamwe raped her again several times.

A few days after the rape she felt unwell and thought that it was because of hunger and the rape which had been so sadistically forced on her by so many men. At the time Umotoni knew nothing about pregnancy because the rape was the first time she had sexual intercourse.

Not realizing that she could be pregnant, Umotoni continued to think that the illness was related to the rape. Once she found out, she felt intensely downhearted. If she had had knowledge on how to abort, she would have done that. It was very difficult for her to accept that she was pregnant from the Intarahamwe. Umotoni agonized and worried about how she could raise a child of a man she never loved and was depressed. At the same time, Umotoni was continually on the move, fleeing from the gunshots that kept going off all around them. People were dying everywhere, especially at roadblocks. She followed others who were fleeing and was not afraid of being killed.

*"There could not be more death than being raped by many unknown men"*, she says.

After a long time of being on the run, Umotoni found herself in the house of an old woman in Gisenyi. She had gone there searching for food. After the woman gave her something to eat, she allowed her to stay with her.

When the war got worse they both fled together to Congo. It was in the refugee camp in Congo that Umotoni gave birth to her firstborn. She then developed malnutrition because of the dreadful living conditions. In 1995, helped by the UN Refugee Agency, Umotoni returned with her daughter to Rwanda. She went to live with her uncle's family in Bugesera and reunited with her mother who had recently come back from the bush. Her mother did not recognize her because she was half dead. Umotoni was hospitalized for a long time because of malnutrition.

While she was at the hospital, her mother took care of her. This helped her to tell that she had been gang raped and that she had given birth to a child of the Intarahamwe. They continued to live at the uncle's place until the mother was given a house in a group of newly built houses for poor and vulnerable people.

Fifteen years later, the uncle who had been supporting them passed away and their living conditions started to deteriorate because neither Umotoni nor the mother was working. They also did not have anywhere to cultivate. Because of that, Umotoni started cohabiting with a man with whom she then had the second child. Truly, she doesn't love him but accepted him because he brought them food after her uncle's death.

Umotoni has long been depressed, hating her firstborn and suffering from persistent headaches. She always felt anxious and had difficulties sleeping and suffered from back pains and sexually transmitted infections. Umotoni still doesn't know the identities of the men who raped her, which causes her much sorrow. Perhaps she could have found out something about the Interahamwe who hurt her through the Gacaca courts, but she did not actively participate in Gacaca because she felt she had nothing to say. The first time that she participated in Gacaca, it seemed as if her head was going to explode. This happened when men started explaining how they had killed her little brother, who was five years old at the time. Umotoni felt particular anguish when the Interahamwe explained how they killed him, and said that her brother had begged them not to kill him because he promised that he would no longer be a Tutsi. As they continued to elaborate on this, she felt immeasurable grief in her heart. They also said that they threw her father and the big brother into the latrine and killed them by throwing stones at them. These killers' statements were addressed to her mother. After a while Umotoni felt her head getting hot and started losing her mind.

While listening to that, she thought about what had happened to her, and was afraid that the rapists might repeat what they had done to her before in the Gacaca court. Umotoni felt deep pain on hearing the killers describe the deaths of her family members. While they were talking she couldn't sit still, she did not know what to do or where to look. Umotoni left Gacaca before the end of the session and went back home. She felt intense sadness, anger and grief. She was confused while her head felt very painful. She was nauseous but was not able to vomit. At that point Umotoni decided not to attend any other Gacaca sessions because what she heard while there was too troubling.

Even though attending Gacaca was difficult for her, hearing the perpetrators tell the truth about the way her siblings were killed and where they had been thrown helped her bury them in dignity. That relieved her heart and she felt that she should forgive them. If she didn't, she would be the one continuing to suffer. So she forgave them and as a result was able to talk to them. But the confidence she has in them is no longer complete. Their relationship cannot be like it was before the genocide.

Gacaca brought Rwandans together and it facilitated communication between Hutus and Tutsis. It has helped the genocide killers ask for pardon. Survivors felt relieved after hearing more about the death of their loved ones and where to find their remains. As a result, some survivors, like Umotoni, forgave the killers of their relatives. For her, justice has been done because the killers were imprisoned. But still, there are those who are in prison but refuse to accept the sin committed against other families. What remains to be done by Gacaca is to pay back their property that was looted. The courts must review all cases of looted property, identify in which cases looting was carried out by people who are so poor that they are unable to refund the damage.

In those cases, the courts might be able to take responsibility for the necessary refunds. Due to all these sorrows, Umutoni often experienced severe psychological problems, especially during the commemoration period. One of the symptoms is feeling like something is walking inside her head. She avoids going to church while genocide commemoration ceremonies are held; instead Umutoni hides in her bed. In April 2012 however, Umotoni did not suffer from *ihahamuka*. She only experienced headaches. Because of various methods of training and counseling, she's slowly managing to cope with her suffering a little bit better. In terms of support, AVEGA helped her treat the rape-related sexually transmitted infections, as well as providing trauma counseling. Since the AVEGA headquarters are located in Kigali, which is relatively far from where she lives, the AVEGA counselor referred her to an Ibuka counselor at the Nyamata health centre, where she could continue benefitting from individual trauma counseling. This kind of support reduced her headaches and helped her forgive the killers. After forgiving them, it felt as though her heart was released. While Umotoni was following the counseling sessions, the counselor connected her with the Kanyarwanda Association, which is now sponsoring her firstborn. Umotoni was then invited to take part in a forum of women who have children born out of rape. After participating for three days, she was able to disclose to her daughter how she was conceived. This helped stop her daughter's relentless questioning about who her father was. It was good to tell her daughter the truth, because before Umotoni was always transferring her anger and sadness onto her. She saw her as the source of her suffering. As a result of being trained by Kanyarwanda, Umotoni started to take care of her. This had a positive impact on her. She improved somewhat in her studies. Later, when Kanyarwanda provided some money for income generating activities to its members, they formed a group of women who visit each other and bring their children born out of rape together. As a group, they visit two members per month. They then eat together, chat and pray.

When Umotoni was still benefitting from the support given by FARG, she was able to buy mutual health insurance for her children. However, Umotoni is no longer on the list of beneficiaries for this support. Even though she benefitted from trauma counseling, she remained anxious. As such, she continued to consult trauma counseling services, because she wanted to feel secure like others. Once she went to the African Evangelical Enterprise (AEE), which resulted in an invitation to follow trauma counseling and reconciliation training. During that training Umotoni met a lot of people like her, who had many problems. One of these, a woman, later invited her to join socio therapy. There, she met women who had also been raped during the genocide. It was the first time for her to sit with old women as a group and talk about these secret issues.

When she decided to follow all socio therapy sessions, it was in the expectation of continuing to talk to other women, to cry and to smile. What made her happy was that they were the same and they all had the same bad experiences. So when she started talking in the group everyone listened. Today she's happy because Umotoni found what she had hoped for.

Because they knew each other, she did not feel any of the usual fear. Meeting other women helped her to be open and talk honestly. She appreciated the exchanges and discussions they had together. After speaking out her sadness, she felt her problems decreasing. Umotoni had never been able to like her firstborn before. After joining socio therapy, she accepted her and loved her. She treats her better now, and always tries to help. Before she felt shame because of the rapes, but since participating in socio therapy she accepted herself and no longer feels ashamed. She was also able to forgive her siblings and her father's killers.

Some of the physical problems, such as the nausea and headaches, disappeared. She now lives in peace with her neighbors and her relationships with other people have also changed for the better. Before, when she had a problem with someone, Umotoni used to keep it inside her heart because she was rancorous. The lessons she received from Socio therapy ameliorated this and thus helped her relationships with others. She learnt that to forgive and ask for pardon are two deeply significant things. When you seek pardon, you feel relieved in your heart. And at the same time, when a person who is asked to forgive offers that pardon, he/she also feels released and the relationship becomes better. Because her behavior changed while participating in socio therapy, her husband's behavior also changed. Before, they communicated badly with each other and sometimes fought.

He squandered all his salary away at the local bar. What saddened Umotoni most was when the husband used to say that he is only working for her daughter born out of rape. Socio therapy helped her get closer to him and to talk to him without using bad words. Learning more and more from socio therapy, Umotoni was able to be more humble with him and she started to respect him. Now, when he has money, he gives her some of it. He no longer spends his nights drinking and he does not insult her the way he used to. Her husband asked her for forgiveness and she forgave him. The relationship was restored thanks to good communication. They now plan everything that they will do at home together. She also now has serenity in her house.

Umotoni has become free in her heart. The socio therapy group is like her family. The older women take care of her. Looking at the future, she expects to do some small business whenever she receives a small amount of money. Umotoni hopes that one day she can sell offspring from the goat which she received from the socio therapy program, and then have enough to further invest in that small business. Umotoni is worried about finding her own house; it is her only burden now.

*"I shared my story here in order to inform other women who are like me that healing is possible. Wherever you are, do not feel guilty. I advise all women to get together, sit somewhere in an intimate place and share your sadness. After being listened to and sharing advice, every woman will feel strength and hope for the future."*

## Uwamulinzi Survives the genocide

Uwamulinzi was 11years when the genocide started. His parents had nine children but she's the only survivor and lives without anybody to turn to. It was the 7th April 1994, early morning when news broke that the President of Rwanda had been killed in the plane crash. Her father told them the news and said that they were going to die because they were Tutsi. Uwamulinzi's mother was sick that she could not move then. After some hours they heard people singing songs that *"We should kill them all"*. Her mother told them to leave and that she would remain behind to protect the house and the properties. Uwamulinzi and the brothers begged her to come with them but she refused and they left. Uwamulinzi never left with the others because she wanted to stay close to her mother, so she hid herself in the neighbor's home where she could still see her mother.

Mean while a group of men with headgears made of leaves carrying clubs were entering people's houses including their home. She heard her mother crying out for help as others were taking out what they wanted from the house. She started crying and wanted to run to her mother but they stopped her because they would kill her too. She stayed and watched all that took place. First they brought her mother out of the house; she was bleeding because they had hit her with tree branches. They started beating her with the sticks while her father was locked inside the house.

Another militia man came and asked them not to waste time on one person because they had many to kill before night came. Uwamulinzi saw the killers slashing off her mother's head and others burnt her father inside the house. It was raining and there were screams all around the village with houses burning and people running to save their lives. Uwamulinzi left the house because the killers were even checking the houses of the Hutu thinking that they had kept the Tutsi inside.

She went to the bush for fear of being found in the Hutu's house. She spent the whole day without eating and all the rain had made her wet. She was with other Tutsis who had escaped to save life. The killers came with dogs to hunt humans and got them from a thick bush were Uwamulinzi and others were hiding. They had captured other Tutsi and they were all made to sit in the field where they were collecting them. After some time they had got many in number and the killers started killing using the Machete. They started with men first and Uwamulinzi was spared with other children and the women. Those who were resisting to be cut were killed in a bad way. As they were fighting, they had to chop off the legs and arms and put them a side and later after the other killers could finish them by hitting their heads with hard tree branches. By then Uwamulinzi had lost feelings after seeing what was going on. It was like she was in a dream that she couldn't awake from.

They raped women and girls in the bush around the fields. Uwamulinzi was also among those they abused sexually. She felt ill and wanted to die then. The other girls and women were killed after using them while Uwamulinzi was spared because the killer wanted to use her whenever he needed to meet his desires sexually. She endured years of torment since the genocide, fear and social pressure trapped him to an abusive relationship and HIV infection. The man took her to a refugee camp pretending that he was helping her but always came and raped her. She ran with different people in search for safety, children, men, women, grandfathers and mothers, were struck with the machete, pangas and clubs. As they felt down those with energy continued running but they were surrounded by heaps of mutilated bodies. Uwamulinzi didn't know why she was being chased or mistreated all that way but she felt that she to run. Her body was struck by tree branches and machete but could not stop running. She regretted why she didn't stay behind to join the fate of her mother and father. She was raped and abused but still had the courage to move on and that was a shocking price she had to pay in order to survive.

Uwamulinzi run to church in Musambara district because they thought it was safe in the house of God. She found many persons in side and it was almost full. They were cooking from inside and prayed at night God to save them. Two days after she had reached the church, the intarahamwe came in big numbers when they had closed themselves inside and threw grenades on the building. They were holding machete and clubs with nails and stopped all those who were escaping out of the church. She was bleeding on her legs and saw dead bodies and those who were about to die all over the church floor and blood was everywhere. The intarahamwe were pick pocketing those who had died and yet to die. Uwamulinzi and other were in one Conner of the church crying and those dying were also screaming because of the pain. They threw the grenade in the Conner were Uwamulinzi and other were and all went down with their body parts a side, as they were checking the bodies she was still alive and was seeing everything. When they reached her, the killers noticed that she was still alive and decide not to kill her and four others were found still alive. Together they moved to Kabgayi while her leg was cut by grenade. She was thinking of how to survive with one leg and who to live life without parents wondering who would care about her.

She went to Kabgayi where she had a cousin Mugorewera, she was married to a Hutu man. During the early insecurities while Mugorewera was going to school, she was kidnapped and he forced her to marry him. When she got there, the cousin tried to treat her wounds and asked her to leave the next morning because the husband wasn't also a good man. Early morning she had to say good bye to the husband but he asked her to stay that she was safe at his house. He stopped her from leaving and after two days he had turned Uwamulinzi to his second wife and after a week he took both of them to his home village in Butare. She suffered painfulness after the rape; he used to sleep with the cousin but at night in the middle he came used her too. He was beating them all night if they resisted doing what he wanted and threatening to hand them to the militia men to be killed.

Uwamulinzi and the cousin Mugorewera decide to commit suicide to a deep pit where unknown bodies were being dumped. They were stopped by neighbors and saved them from dying. When he got to know about it he beat them as he was saying that until when they die then he will stop the beating. Several times they tried to escape but even had fear to where they could head to. They tried to take cans to go fetch water and then escape but he learnt the plan and stopped them from leaving home again. He had to lock them in the house each time he was leaving. The cousin got very ill and had no treatment that later after three days she died on the bed where she was tied. Uwamulinzi noticed when she tried to call her because both of them were tied separately that they couldn't plan how to escape. When she called her, Mugorewera couldn't respond and when the husband returned, he took out the body and dumped her in the pit. Uwamulinzi was then pregnant and final gave birth in for the first born in May 1995 but never liked the baby and wanted to throw her in the bush but she returned her back. The war was ending, she managed to escape with the baby to her home village but everyone hated her for nurturing a militia's son, and the Uncle used it as an excuse to throw her out of the house and went to a small house. A distant relative often visited her but also needed to use her sexually. She was digging for others to get food and little pay to care about the baby. She had no one to turn to for help but later decided to take the child to the father. She moved back and found out he had moved to Kigali, she went to where they had directed her and she found him, he welcomed them and asked for forgiveness on all what he had done to them before. He asked her to stay and they make a family but Uwamulinzi never wanted.

The man insisted and Uwamulinzi became his wife even after the genocide, she stayed with him against her wishes, because she was ashamed of what everybody who knew her would say about her. The man was unfaithful and in April 2002 he died. She was four months pregnant of the second child and she came to realize she could be infected with AIDs at birth. She was always uncomfortable, she was always ill. She gave birth to big baby but he got thinner as he grew older. She had given birth of three children before the man's death. The oldest is 19. She decided to take an HIV test and learnt that she was positive. This made her revile her past and felt traumatized. Her family comforted her and she had to believe that it wasn't her blame to make her life more miserable. Whenever she thinks of it deeply, she tells her self that she's not the only one but there others in worse situations. The relative took the burden of his children, growing foods that they live on but later died soon after from the cuts she had got from the genocide grenade. ….

Uwamulinzi doesn't cry for justice because its beyond his reface, the horrors of genocide have been reduced to a mere man slaughtering, she says *"No justice can bring back my sanity and life but this should have happened to no human."* She managed to return back home and collected the bones of her parents and buried them and she lucky for that because others don't even know where their relatives are. *"am among the many dead but not buried. I remain as a statement to what happened to a million Rwandese for you and for the world to hear. History has a way of repeating it's self but I hope here it doesn't happen again. By remembering me you remember all the innocent victims yet forgetting me means forgetting what happened then there will be no reason for me to live because I live to bear witness and to tell my testimony."*

# Emerine

Emerine was a fifth year student of the Groope Seolaire Marie Merci of Kibeho at the time the genocide was launched. This was at the time when schools had been closed for Easter holidays apart from hers as she and the rest of the students had remained to catch up on lessons they had missed during the school strikes. Fear and tension started building up the school mostly among the Tutsi students of which Emerine belonged as they watched massacres of Tutsis take place around them like at the Parish of Kibeho, the hospital and the primary school. The massacres in Kibeho hospital went on until the intarahamwe ran out of victims.

This marked the beginning of Emerine's misery and that of her fellow Tutsi students who had stayed back at school. Since they were no more Tutsi to kill around in Kibeho, Emerine and her fellow Tutsi were asked to leave the school and were segregated in the nearby college of Kibeho.

On the 7th of May, it was very early in the morning when they were asked to come out of the dormitory. With no choice and nowhere to escape, 82 boys and girls were shot and hacked to death by the killers who were villagers, gendarmes and worst of all fellow pupils who were once their classmates and friends. They were just eight survivors, Emerine inclusive. Tears run down her eyes as she remembers how she and her friend Uwera Delphine were abducted by their teachers and repeatedly raped. They suffered the depths of human misery and degradation in their effort to stay alive. From the hands of their teachers to the deadly killers, they were tossed like useless creatures which had no say to what was to become of them.

This went on until Emerine got fed up of the situation of being raped every single night by the Hutu killers to survive while also doing hard labour on force. She recalls the day of Saturday morning when she decided to escape the room her and the friends had been locked for days. Unfortunately for Uwera was very weak that she couldn't make it out. For days, Emerine searched her way through bushes and swamps until she reached a primary school and many had gathered for protection by the watchman known as Gervais. She was able to convince him to let her in deceiving him that she had been mistaken for a Tutsi girl by some group of Hutu boys who had been having her captive until her escape from them. She was asked to join those who hid in the laundry room as other areas where already full of people.

It was from this laundry room that Emerine witnessed her worst nightmare that up to now can't erase it from her mind. On the first night of her stay, at around 8pm, the watchman Gervais came in the room that she was next to the laundry where she was hiding. He held a baby barely alive and hardly able to sit up. Since the room was fully occupied by many people and girls between fifteen and twenty years, he left the baby with them expecting them to look after it. Solange, Emerine's classmate was the head of the room and was a Hutu. But she had a bad feeling about the other Tutsi people, she took refugee among them but was only waiting for a time when they would turn against them.

Since the baby was tired, hungry and frightened, she cried the whole night. Solange stood up and shout that she didn't want to hear the cries of the Tutsi baby. She ordered and threatened the watchman Gervais that if he did not kill the baby, she would take him to the killers as an accomplice of the Tutsi. With no choice but to follow orders, Gervais the watchman took the baby and struck her with the machete and the remains were dumped out of the toilet. It was horrible but joyful to Solange and other Hutu who were around, they had turned the place to their hands. Emerine was angered to the point of controlling Solange hoping to put some sense and sympathy in her. However things went for Emerine, Solange and other extremist girls engaged her and tied her up as they waited for the head of the extremist group in Kibeho to hand her over the head of the killers. At 5pm, before the killers returned Emerine had escaped and walked through a bushy path to the rice fields where several dead bodies were lying in pool of blood. It was the killing ground and dumping zone. From where he had escaped she could listen to shout outs for forgiveness. They had started killing all those inside be it girls, boys, young or old. Others were escaping to the bush around but they were shooting them, the few who were lucky had the chance to escape while those caught were used as targeting practice for the young killers.

It was from their where Emerine and another girl survivor got in the hands of women who said to them that they could hide them. They two went to the Hutu house but they were doing as maids for her. They worked from morning to morning and at times they missed food or shared one plate among them for all the day. Emerine remembers washing clothes that had human blood hoping that they were stole from Tutsi persons and ounce they asked food, the woman could tell them to go an feed on the Tutsi bodies on the streets. Emerine got sick and she could no longer work. The woman forced her out of the house saying she had no use any more. She moved to the health centre hoping to find some help, she was lucky to receive some treatment on the orders of a Militia man who later abducted her and forcefully married her.

Every single night at this man's home, Emerine was beaten, dipped in a water bucket and rapped not only by him but also other Hutu men who came around his home. Within a short time she was pregnant and when the Hutu husband learnt about it, he threw her out claiming not to take responsibility of a Tutsi woman. She became homeless and at the risk of being killed by the intarahamwe who were at every Conner. Emerine wandered off moving house to house seeking refugee but no one could open up for her. For days she kept on moving, hiding, and stealing food. This went on until she came across a roadblock of the intarahamwe. They held her captive and the following day the leader of the roadblock called Kaniziyo came and asked her to take the lorry that was carrying other intarahamwe soldiers. Late at night, they reached Kaniziyos' house where there were other women and young girls. During the night, Emerine was briefed on what her new job was to be. Just like the people who had murdered her schoolmates. Emerine was going to become one of them. As early as 6am, Emerine and other girls were ordered to go on roadblocks and wait for orders. There task was to finish off people. She recalls killing a mother with her two daughters under pressure of the Hutu men. She was reluctant when they got to the roadblock where they had to wait the Tutsi people, she was beaten badly that the even the child she was expecting died. But this helped her to stay back whenever others went to the roadblock to kill. On the fifth day at home she was taken together with other girls to a mission on a local church where a large group of Tutsi were hiding. When they reached the killers beaked inside and started to kill, they clubs and ordered to kill too. After that, they asked them to loot the dead bloody bodies and collect the items on the truck they had came with. She was cold at this point and ice and no longer had a heart inside her. She just followed orders as long as it kept her alive and safe, this was her new life although part of her was against it, the only option available was either kill or die.

After weeks of killing and cleaning up from roadblocks, they travelled on trucks to Gisenyi and this was her home area. They had grow from that side and was her birthplace and often came for holidays from school. They reached late at night and camped at the ragional head quarters with other intarahamwe members and leaders. They were given meat and local brew as super and then started getting their weapons ready as they were to raid the next morning. Emerine's victim was her former teacher and her entire family. His house was raid and bombed by the grenade, there were seven children and two women but non survived when the militia got inside and started strucking them with the machete. Without hesitation, Emerine with her club hit the four children to death. She was ordered to finish her teacher who had been cut by the grenade, the teacher pleaded to her but all in vain he wasn't spared. They looted his belongings and continued.

Emerine with the other women and girls moved from house to house killing any Tutsi they came across but deep down Emerine was grieving for killing his own people some were even relatives or friends but it was her only way to live. On the last day of the killings, they came to where she lived. Her mother and two young twins to her sister had moved to that place to hide from the intarahamwe, when she went to ask them to run away her mother denied her to get in the house because she had seen what Emerine had turned to on his people. Other intarahamwe women had come following her but she didn't know. They saw her on the window trying to talk to her mother, they came running saying to her that we are coming to help you if they have locked themselves inside. They found her mother and the twins and burnt them inside the house.

Tears came down her eyes looking on the burning house with her mother inside. At time Emerine couldn't keep around with the killers. She had lost her mother who gave her life that she was striving paying for a high price to keep. She decided to escape despite what could come around or what challenges awaited for her. She didn't know where to turn so she decide to run toward Congo, she passed through shrubs and all her body was scrubbed by tree branches until when got to Congo.

She had got in to another country with no one to turn to unless all those who had managed to find refugee in Congo. She moved to the refugee camp and stayed a week. She went to the Red Cross car and returned to Goma near Rwanda. That's she started to sketch a new life since the genocide was ending. With no money, food, shelter or friends and family except the clothes she was wearing, she resorted to prostitution to earn some money. The first days weren't easy as she was used and not paid. Later after Emerine hocked up with another Congo prostitute who took her in and started working for her. The woman always brought men and slept with her but the pay went to the woman who divided it then but Emerine always took the little share. She was on a tiny bed to rest on, few clothes to wear and two meals a day.

Life moved on she regarded herself as dead person among the alive. Because of the depression and sadness that filled her heart body and soul she resorted to drugs for comfort. Drugs became a companion and it wasn't long that the woman pushed her out as she could no longer manage her. She joined the drug addicts and later started selling them too.

She got involved with the gang leader who later contracted to get married. She got sick and was taken to hospital where she was left with no one to care about her. They run because they thought she was dead. After two days at the hospital, various tests were carried out and she was informed she was HIV positive. They asked her place of origin and when they learnt that she was a Rwandese she was sent back to her country. From there she was pointed out by the survivors that she was among the killers. The RPF took her to Nyamagabe prison where other killers were sentenced but after five years, she confessed and was sent to do community work.

## Valentina's Narrow Death Experience

Valentina was just 16 years of age when the genocide began. Valentina had a brother who was 15years old and both loving parents. The family lived in the northern province of Rwanda and they were a very well respected family because they were rich since they had cattle. In Rwanda the moment you had cows in your family, you would be respected and cattle was taken as a sign of prestige. Valentina's father was a farmer and the mother was a house wife who used to take good care of her family and household. Valentina's father's relatives had been clearly wiped out during the genocide that started way back in the early 1959. So Valentina had neither cousins nor relatives on his father's side by the time of 1994, but she had a few relatives on her mother's side.

On April 6, 1994, Juvenal Habyarimana the president of Rwanda then was killed when his airplane, also carrying the Presidente of neighboring country Burundi, Cyprien Ntaryamira, was shot down close to Kigali International Airport. His assassination ignited ethnic tensions in the region and helped spark the Rwandan Genocide. The government soldiers and the presidential guard blamed the assassination on the Tutsis who were a minority ethnic group in Rwanda. The Tutsis had been a target of the genocide from way back as far as 1950's due to the ideologies created by whites who came to colonize this tiny country. The government soldier quickly swung into action and they set up road blocks everywhere most especially on the roads leading in and out of Kigali the capital of Rwanda. The genocide supporting radio called RTLM started reading out Tutsis and moderate Hutu families to be killed and these even included prominent leaders in the Rwanda like Agathe Uwilingiyimana, one of the most influential women in Rwandan history. She was the prime minister of Rwanda who was brutally killed and her 10 Belgium body guards by the well armed presidential guard.

In Valentina's region the genocide started exactly 10 days after the president's plane had been shot down. It was started by the men working in the market and they started by killing all the Tutsi women who had gone for shopping of foodstuffs, and thereafter militia men known as interhamwe a Kinyarwanda word meaning *"we attack together"* and the military came to the region to carry out their given assignments of killing all the innocent Tutsi and moderate Hutu families. Terror then fell upon ever Tutsi family in the region including Valentina's family. The Tutsi families started alerting each other so as to look for a solution and to escape the genocide but wasn't made any easy as road blocks were being erected all over the country. Valentina remembers that day they never had any meal because each and everyone was scared and they wanted to find a way forward. Valentina's father got a hold of the all the valuables they could handle and some hard cash so that they could move. After he collected some small stuff in the house and told his family to move and look for safety somewhere far and secure. One of their Hutu friends found them and told them it would be very difficult to pass by the roadblocks which were being manned by the interhamwe militia, and continued to tell them that they should avoid using the highways.

He told them to be able to pass by the road blocks they should first flash their identity cards and that if they showed Tutsis they could be killed on the spot, but Hutus could pass through the road blocks without any questioning. Valentina's dad thought for the moment and told them that the only safe place to be at the time would be the church and so they embarked on their way to the church. They thought that the moment they reached the church their lives would be spared but unfortunately this was not the case since there were also some mass killings in churches but they didn't hear about them since the radios were busy in sighting violence into crowds to go ahead and kill all Tutsis in the country. Valentina thought that since they were in the house of GOD they couldn't be executed but she says that the killers didn't have any respect for the house of GOD. When the family reached the church they found a lot of people who had come to look for refuge in the church. The joy and merry making of being alive didn't last that long because on the same night that they reached the church, a group of over 30 militia men mixed with the government soldiers surrounded the whole church and they didn't allow anyone to come in or outside the church premises. The militia head then set a message to the people who were inside the compound of the church and also the church that they had to have their last supper and also have their last prayers on that night that things would dramatically change in the morning as the head of the hit squad was busy laughing and enjoying his terror message on a megaphone speaker. The people who were outside and inside the church didn't take the words seriously as they thought that they could be protected by God and that the men who were waiting outside the gate of the church would not kill them inside the church. The refugees in the church took their supper and discussions continued whether the militias were really serious about what they said. Some other refugees who had made their way to the church gate were beaten with heavy clubs and others were hacked by machetes and they died instantly, Valentina looked at the men who were carrying out the killings outside the gate and they appeared so heartless and they carried out their killings so happily without any consideration for human life. The militia and the army camped outside the church gate and there were lorries which again shipped in more men to come and re-enforce the ones that were already there. Valentina says that a few people were scared and the others were not even bothered by the presence on the soldiers outside the gate. Valentina says she never slept thinking of what would happen the next day. The refugees then mobilized a group of some strong men and they put them on guard that whole night to watch the actions of the militia. Which they did very well but early in the morning the events suddenly changed. In the morning at 6am when the sun had come out, the leader of the militia who was also the mayor of Valentina's region came and gave his men orders to finish off all Tutsis in the church. The refugees then started getting scared. The mayor added on saying that Tutsis were "*Inzoka*" a Kinyarwanda word meaning a snake and that the only way to kill a snake is by hitting it on the head and so the Tutsis in the church had to be killed that way. The militia and the army were armed with big clubs, grenades, guns, machetes, knives and other things that would be used to finish off someone's life but the refugees were armed with a few stick and stones which couldn't even defend them from half of the militia.

In the militia that was outside, Valentina knew almost all of them and gazed at them and they looked back at her with an evil look like they were going to do something foolish. Among the people she knew was a 56 year old man whose children studied with Valentina at the same school and they were her close friends but their dad was also outside the gate waiting to finish them off. The leader of the militia then told the terrified crowd that whoever submitted their valuables and also hard cash would be spared and that they could be forgiven and they could be left to go away with their families. People were scared at first but when a few people submitted their valuables the militia told them to step besides them. The people who thought they could be spared were the ones that were killed first showing the others that nothing they could do would buy their lives and the hatred the Hutus had over the Tutsis. The people who were killed at first included Valentina's dad who had gone to bribe the militia to spare him and his family. Valentina remembers that his father was hit with a club on the head that cracked his skull leading to his death. Valentina says she cried but the men did stop there, they also hacked him several times with a machete and cut him into pieces which they threw at their savage dogs to eat. This time the whole crowd at the church was scared at the way the militia killed the people that attempted to buy their lives out and they wondered what would be done to the ones who didn't have any money. Valentina says she held her mother's hand and her mum held her brother's hand. Their mother then told them that if they had to die they had to die as a family but the two children looked in misery as their mother talked about death. Valentina said she wasn't scared of death but was scared about the way she would die. Some of the men then threw a few stones to the militia to keep them outside the gate and also to slow their advance. After most of the people who were outside the church had entered the church and a few were left outside the militia fired at the people who had kept them outside and they were killed on the spot and then the mayor ordered that no one should be spared and that each and everyone had to be killed, without sparing the kids and women. The people who were still outside were brutally killed some by clubs and others were hacked several times with machetes and there was no one left alive outside. The people in the church where Valentina and her family were closed the entrance to the church and they put their obstacles at the entrance to make it difficult for the militia to get into the church. Some strong men went ahead to hold the door with their hands with all their might but the militia outside the doors were heard laughing at the people who locked the doors. The second in command of the militia then shouted at the people who were inside the gate to open the door willingly or they could force their way inside, but there plea fell on deaf ears as no one was willing to let them come inside and the leader of the church parish cried out for mercy as he refused to open the door but no one was willing to listen to him. The militia saw that it was getting late and so they had to blow up all the church entrances. They threw grenades at the church entrances and the grenades also hurt and killed many people in the church including those that were holding the doors closely. The men that held the doors for sometime were hurt very bad and some even were blown up into small pieces and there body parts spread all over the church. There were screams all over the church as the people were crying out for mercy.

 The militia at last had managed to come into the church and they started organizing the crowds into groups and they separated them as follows: men, women and children. The militia then discussed the order in which they could kill the people inside the church. They finally agreed and they were to start with the children first. Some of the babies were removed from their mothers and then thrown against the wall. They died instantly. Some other children were then hacked by machetes, hit several times to their death and the other young children above 5years were put in a small church and grenade were thrown onto them and after the blasts Valentina says you couldn't hear any more screams as the children had all been killed. At one time they even got a pregnant woman and cut her stomach open to remove the child that she carried. It was still a fetus but they killed it along with its mother. There is another pregnant mother that they killed by passing a sharp pointed long hooked stick into her uterus to remove the baby. The woman screamed in pain but the men were just enjoying what they were doing. The poor woman died of over bleeding and everyone was one scared for their lives. The next people to be killed were then the youth who included Valentina and her brother. Valentina's mother pulled her children to her as they were taking them away but one of the militia attacked her and cut off her hand. Her children cried in pain but then another militia hit Valentina with a machete that cut through her head next to her ear and then her brother was hit with a club that had nails at the end. It cut and burst the 15year old's brain, Valentina's brother died on the spot. Valentina pretended as though she was dead and she was spared thinking she was dead and by the time they were done with

Valentina, it was already late so the men had to go and rest outside the church where their  leader brought for them alcohol and food for the job well done. At night Valentina's mum crawled to Valentina and held her hand as she cleaned her wound. When the militia came in Valentina's mum quickly ran and fall back into her position so that the militia couldn't realize that she was still alive as they would immediately kill her. The militia at the church never raped anyone inside the church as they used to say that the women were beasts and that they deserved to die leaving no descendants. The killings at the church went on for four consecutive days without anyone stopping the killings as the people who had to stop the killings were busy advocating and encouraging the killings. On the second day they killed all the women mercilessly without any consideration for human life. Valentine could wake up at night, she could see all the dead bodies of the women brutally killed some were just hanged and most of them were hacked several times with machetes and so was Valentina's mother, Valentina says she was hacked several times until she lost her life. On some days they could come and collect the bodies of the dead and then killed the ones that had survived. The militia on the fourth day came and took Valentina in a room where they were dumping or depositing off the dead bodies, since she knew that if they caught her she could be killed she went ahead and hid among the dead bodies. Some of them had even started to rot and the dogs and hyenas came along in the night to eat them.

After the militia had killed the men they started checking the bodies and killed all the survivors but they didn't want to touch in the dead bodies that had already started rotting because they said they were smelling. Some of the people that had survived were taken to the Sunday school where they were burnt alive and whoever escaped was shot dead on the spot. After depositing off the bodies the militia then fled the scene and this time they never came back. Fortunately Valentina survived and she crawled out of the heap of bodies to the surface and went outside the church where she found some other survivors. She was very weak, malnourished and had a deep infected wound on the head but she didn't feel anything as she only wanted to die. The survivors who were strong enough prepared the food and they fed her but she couldn't digest it as the food was also half cooked. Some of the survivors died due to the bleeding of the wounds they had. They kept on hiding in the mass graves until when the RPF soldiers and the doctors without borders came into the region and captured it and that's when they came and got Valentina and other survivors and they were given all the care they needed. The RPF was a force that wanted to stop the genocide and managed to some extent. Valentina was very malnourished and she needed a lot of good and healthy food to survive which she got in the RPF camp and she managed to survive against all odds. She says if she had the means to stop the genocide she would not let it happen anywhere else in the world and she's now an activist against genocide in the world. She's also a guide at the memorial centre that was set up at the church.

# Umunyana's Tale

Umunyana was a young beautiful lady aged 18years in 1994. Her whole family was finished off as they were about to go in for the Easter celebrations. They had gathered as they usually do during Easter period or holidays. Her whole family was brutally killed. She was born in a Christian family and she believes she survived the genocide because of God's presence and guidance. Umunyana's family was that of a more peasantry background and they had their home isolated on a hill. They were seated having dinner on the night of April 06th when they suddenly heard a lot of gunshots, the family was very scared. Their father quickly turned on his radio receiver to get to know what was really happening and also to know what really caused the gunshots and the explosions. When he turned on his radio the first station he got announced that the president's plane had been shot down by some unknown people as it made its way on the run way at Kanombe international airport. The radio never established who really shot down the plane but blamed it on the advancing RPF soldiers and their collaborators who were the Tutsis. The radio announced that the Hutus must fight for their rights and that they should not allow any Tutsi to take over power. Umunyana's dad kept the radio on throughout the night because he wanted to have all the updates of the country at the time. The family enjoyed their dinner and Umunyana went to bed and so did her mum but they left their father still listening to the radio as he wanted to know the updates. After nearly three hours of Umunyana sleeping, their father woke them up and told them that the country was in turmoil as the prime minister had also been killed but this time by the presidential guard. Her only crime was that she was a Tutsi. The extremist radio began to read out all the names of the people they called collaborators of the RPF. Umunyana says she herself couldn't sleep because of all the gunshots and explosions that hit the area. Her father then went and closed the main gate leading to their home and also tightly locked the doors to his home. Umunyana's family belonged to the Tutsis ethnic group so there father thought that they could also become a target for the government soldiers and also the militia men that were trained and had been deployed by the interim president then. Umunyana's father called his few friends and they told him that some of the friends they used to share with a beer every evening were hunting them down like a prey running for its life. Umunyana's father became even more scared than before and thought of running away with his family but again a friend called him up and told him that road blocks had been erected all over the country and that it was very difficult for one to make his way past the roadblocks as one had to flash an identity card to pass through. Umunyana's dad was very deep in thought as Umunyana explains and he was thinking of what would happen next to him and his family. He then decided that he will not leave the country and that he wouldn't leave his home. Every morning Umunyana's father received new family members from his side and also from his wife's side and some few family friends. This was because their house was strategically located in an isolated area far from the road and also far from society. The area where they lived was considered a safe zone because it had been infested with tsetse flies and a lot of mosquitoes and the government had forgotten this area and therefore the genocide took a lot of time to reach the area. Umunyana's dad had hired two shamber boys to work on his farm and also help him cultivate his land. He hired them for months before the president's plane was shot down. The two boys were Rwandan Hutus and they disliked the family but the family was very welcoming to them and they were also given whatever they wanted by Umunyana's father. Umunyana characterized her father as being welcoming and a very social person but the boys just had a lot of hate towards him because he was rich compared to them.

The family spent about a week without any problems coming to their home and so he continued letting other people into the house and there reached a time when the food was scarce and so they had to go out and look for food. Instead of the father going, he instead decided that he could send the two shamber boys to the market to bring him and his new family food. The two boys agreed to go to the market because for them they couldn't arouse any suspicions since they were Hutus and they didn't have any problem passing by the road blocks. Instead of the boys going to the market, they just went to inform the militia that there were a lot of "*cockroaches*" hiding at their boss's home, they stroked a deal with the militia which included also taking their boss's property and the militia said it was okay. The militia then organized a full van full of well equipped militia men accompanied by the two boys who were directing the vehicle where the house was. The militia had a few problems climbing up the hill with their vehicle and that's when Umunyana's father finally noticed that something wasn't right because there wasn't any path/road in which a car could pass to get to house and the only passage way was also muddy. Umunyana's dad quickly told all the people in the house that had come to seek for refuge to quickly go and hide in the attic where they usually kept their old stuff and it was big enough for the number that was available. The boys had left the gate open so Umunyana's father quickly ran and closed it with padlocks. When the men were able to reach the gate the boys thought that it was still open so they hurriedly came and pushed the gate unknowingly. On realizing that the gate was closed the militia ordered the boys to quickly climb up and get the gate open. The boys then quickly climbed the gate and went ahead and tried to open the door but it had padlocks. The two boys then came to the house door and pleaded for their boss to open the door so that they could come in and the only thing Umunyana's dad asked the boys was whether they had brought the food he had sent them and they told him that they couldn't find any food as the market was closed. Umunyana's dad was quick to establish that the two boys were lying, on realizing that their trick hadn't worked, they quickly ran and told the militia who were waiting outside for the gate to be opened that there were some padlocks at the gate. The leader of the militia was furious and so he ordered that the gate be blown off by a grenade which the militia did forcing their way into the gate. The angry militia then came, banged the door of the house and ordered for the door to be opened. Umunyana's father who was also very furious and fearless after realizing that it was the militia, told everyone in the attic to keep quiet and he decide to go ahead and open the door of the house, after opening the door, the militia were rather rude and they just pushed him out of their way and came into the house without saying anything. The two boys who had betrayed the family instead stayed outside due to the guilt they had against Umunyana's father. The militia started interrogating the father and asked him where he had hid his family and all the "*cockroaches*" he was hiding but he kept on denying that there was no one else in the house apart from him. The militias were quick and they started searching the house but didn't find any trace of the alleged people he was hiding. One of the men then hit him with a gun butt on the head and he started bleeding but he couldn't reveal where the refugees he was hiding were. The militia continued their beating and the leader asked the boys whether they knew any secret hide out where the people could be and one of the boys came out and said he knew. All the people in the attic were very scared at what could happen to them if they were caught by the angry militia. The militia then escorted the boy to the attic and told him to open it but it was locked. Instead of the militia calling for the father to open, they just blew it up and continued their way inside the attic. After opening the attic there were a lot of people more especially women and their children and they were ordered out with their hands on their heads. They then told all of them to kneel on their knees with little resistance. The militia then separated the men from the women and children which was done quickly without any resistance because whoever resisted was quickly shot on the spot. The men were taken to the dining room and told to put their heads face down and the women and children also stayed in another separate room and so did Umunyana and her mother. The militia stated beating up the men but Umunyana's father quickly came out and told the militia that he could give them cows and everything they needed in order to spare the lives of everyone that was inside the house and the militia gave him only five minutes. After the five minutes were done the militia asked for the money and he only had 35,000frw Rwandan francs which at the time was a lot of money but only told him that that money was only for two "*cockroaches*". Umunyana's father was told to pick out the people that he had saved and he pointed at his wife and child. The militia just laughed and got hold of Umunyana's mum who was very beautiful. The militia then started raping Umunyana's mum in the presence of her father. The three men who raped her then continued and wanted to rape Umunyana but her father came forward to defend her but he was again hit on the head with a gun butt. And the men continued to rape Umunyana and other women consequently. Umunyana's vagina was completely torn apart and it was heavily bleeding. Umunyana says the whole house was filled with blood and one would think that there was some cleaning or red painting in the house as many people were being beaten with sticks and others had already been shot dead and their bodies were scattered all over. The children were then locked in the master bedroom and it was set ablaze. The innocent children screamed in pain and misery and the only thing one could do was to also cry for them as nothing could be done. Umunyana had never seen such heartless people in her life. There was one baby that had been hid in the cupboard, the baby suddenly burst into tears and started crying. On realizing that there was a baby crying, the militia pulled it out and carried it as though the militia wanted it to stop crying which the baby suddenly did. Everyone was happy at the way the man had handled the baby but this happiness didn't last that long as the baby was finally made to laugh and as the baby laughed the militia quickly got her and threw her with a lot of might against the wall and the baby died instantly. Everyone looked at the man as he celebrated and laughed. The baby's head had been completely smashed. The militia then went onto the men and they started shooting at them aimlessly and most of them got wounds but this wasn't enough as the militia then came in with their machetes and they started hacking the injured men most of them to their death. The militia then came to Umunyana's dad and hacked him several times in the neck area and he died looking at Umunyana who was traumatized at all the brutality the men had carried out. One of the militia then came and pulled out Umunyana from the rest and told her if she wanted to survive she had to be his mistress. She had no way out but to agree and leave with him as the rest of her loved ones were wiped out. There were some few survivors but all of them were killed as the two boys were just looking at the wealth the old man had left and all that was taken by them. Umunyana was then forcefully taken to become a mistress for a person that had raped her and other women earlier her mother inclusive. She says she was raped everyday in the 6 months she was with the man and at once even had a baby but she wasn't able to conceive because of her broken uterus. When the leader of the militia realized that this man had a Tutsi mistress, he quickly came to the house where Umunyana was living and they wanted to kill her but when they got home, Umunyana was still down because of the suicide attempt she had made on her life but failed. Umunyana said she wanted to relieve herself from all the misery the man had brought to her and she says she used to cry a lot whenever she thought of her family. After the man rescued her, he beat her up real bad and left her for death but the leader of the militia pulled out his machete and struck her on the arm and leg. Umunyana says she cried in pain but the leader of the militia ordered that she be dumped in the public dumping area. The men then carried Umunyana's body and put it on a pickup truck and they drove off to the site not knowing that the RPF soldiers had laid an ambush for them which they eventually fell in. After the men had dumped Umunyana, the RPF soldiers quickly came out of their cover and they pointed their guns at the militia who wanted to escape but were all shot down and killed. The RPF soldiers carried Umunyana to their car and she was taken to a camp and she was given the necessary treatment, but the sad news she had to endure was that her arm had to be cut off because it was hurt so bad and they couldn't do nothing to stop it from being cut, the doctors went forth and told her that if it wasn't cut off in time, it would lead to rotting and so she really had to live with the reality of not having a hand. The doctors also told her that she had HIV/AIDS and that she couldn't have babies. They took her for counseling and she was able to coup with all the challenges. When the government was overthrown she quickly returned to her father's property and found there the two boys who she immediately reported to the authorities and they were arrested and convicted. Umunyana says that she always has dreams of her and her parents and she wakes up and finds no one around for her. She recently looked for the remains of her parents and gave them a decent burial.

# Assumpta's Fateful Story

Assumpta is a survivor of the 1994 Rwandan Genocide against the Tutsis by the Hutu. Assumpta was born in a Tutsi family and by the time of the genocide she was18 years old and she still remembers most of the awful things that happened to her during the period of insecurity and turmoil. Assumpta tells a story that she had kept to herself for years but she's pressured to tell it out because of some individuals or people that say that the acts of genocide were not committed or carried out in Rwanda. She tells her story in a sorrowful state as she explains.

Assumpta is the only surviving member of her family. She is a victim of rape, constant beatings, hacking, and so much more atrocities. On April 06th when the president's of the republic of Rwanda was killed in a plane crash, Kigali, city the capital city of Rwanda, became the most unsecure place to be for all Tutsis. Interhamwe militia were organized and Assumpta says that two big buses carrying the interhamwe militia armed with machetes, guns, grenades, clubs, knives and very many other weapons designed to take away someone's life. The big buses arrived in their town that night as though they were being deployed for a mission. The *"Interhamwe"* a Kinyarwanda word meaning *"we hit together"* was a political youth wing from the president's party which was called MRND. The political youth wing wasn't only taught politics but also the art of war and killing techniques. When the militia reached Assumpta's town, there were screams from everywhere and people were calling for help. Assumpta remembers that that night they were having a family dinner and most of their family members were around and they were all having a nice time up to when they heard the screams. The meal never continued because each and everyone was very scared of what was going on outside in the neighborhood. Immediately Assumpta's father switched on the radio to at least get a glimpse of what was happening in Kigali and the whole of Rwanda at that time. On switching it on the radio that had first class news was instead telling people to look for "*cockroaches*" all over the country and crash them. The radio that was supposed to give news was busy in sighting violence into people. That is also when the radio said that the president's plane had been shot down by unknown assailants as it made its way to the runway on Kanombe airport, Kigali's main airport that time and even today. The radio started reading out Tutsi families on the radio telling the militia to go and kill those families of "Inyezi" meaning "cockroaches" and that cockroaches had to be killed by extermination. Assumpta's father fell silent thinking of what would happen next. Each and everyone at home was looking at each other with the saddest face they could put on because they had also heard their name being read over the radio and the militia who heard specific targets were already in town and ready to carry out their missions. The father then told the whole family that they should first pray and then they continue to look for safety somewhere else. The family then converged together, had their prayers and everything was one set to move out.

Assumpta's mother had a broken leg and she couldn't travel long distances and for her she just decided she would stay at home and wait for whatever would come her way. Assumpta's father told the rest of the family to move avoiding all the major highways and roads saying that all the roads leading in and outside town had roadblocks erected by the presidential guards and manned by the interhamwe militia. Assumpta stayed with her father trying to convince their mother to move with them but all this was in vain as she couldn't even move towards the door. Their mother was instead telling them to move and go away before the militia come. Assumpta's father pleaded and all this was in vain as it fell on deaf ears. Assumpta's father went and tightly locked the door and he helped Assumpta's mum up to her room and he told her to tightly lock the doors. Assumpta and the father then decided to move together but to a nearby place right next to their home where Assumpta's father could see his wife clearly. Gunshots and people screaming for their life were being heard and this time it was in the neighborhood. The other family members had already fled the house but unfortunately they never made it past the roadblocks that were erected everywhere. One of the family members came back to tell Assumpta's father that all the members were captured and hacked by machetes and others were being beaten by heavy clubs that had even nails. The family member, who survived, survived because he was moving at a slow pace and was able to detect danger a far distance. The other family member joined Assumpta and her father in the hiding. Assumpta's father didn't want to lose a sight of the house he had left his wife. Suddenly a van carrying the militia arrived at the house where Assumpta's mother was and the three that had hid started getting scared for the life of the person that they had left inside. The leader of the group came forward and started knocking at the door. He knocked for a while and nobody answered the door. The militias then were ordered to knock down the wooden door. They kicked it but it was so hard so they decided to get a grenade and they threw it against the door and it opened wide without any resistance. They went into the house and they saw nobody inside and they came back and told their commander who told them to run back and search the whole house very well and that's when they found one locked door. Assumpta and the rest heard the sound of a grenade and that was used to get her mother out of the room she was hiding.

They started taking whatever was valuable and they also took hard cash because Assumpta saw them counting the money they had found in the house. They later came out dragging Assumpta's mother holding her by the hair. They dragged her to where the commander was standing, the commander then rested his leg on Assumpta's mother's leg which was injured. The poor woman cried out loud as she was in pain. The other militias were then laughing while kicking the her in the stomach. The commander ordered his subjects to strip Assumpta's mum naked which they did and they were enjoying as though they didn't have women or children. The commander seemed mature but he was heartless. He then went ahead and started raping Assumpta's mother in the presence on the father and the other relative. She was crying in pain and Assumpta also remembers that her father also started crying as though he wanted to do something about it. The second in command also wanted to rape her but to their surprise Assumpta's father got out of the blue and told them to stop their atrocities. Assumpta also wanted to follow the father but was held down by the uncle she was hiding with. Before Assumpta's father came any closer, he was shot in the leg but still continued to the scene where they were holding his wife. The commander then asked who he was while stepping in his bullet wound and he explained who he was and they found out that it was the person that they were looking for so they quickly knew that the woman they had raped was his wife. They said that they could even do even worse things to her in his presence. The militia then raped her in front of the husband again and for that time Assumpta was crying and she looked at her future without parents practically impossible but it was the reality. A militia held Assumpta's father's head and showed him clearly the scene of raping his wife. After all the rape, the men then picked up broken bottles and sticks and started inserting them into the wife's vagina and it burst as the husband saw everything. He was being beaten and kicked by the militia who were very happy and were laughing saying that their mission was a success. Assumpta's father asked the militia to kill him first but they didn't and they just went ahead and hacked Assumpta's mum with a machete on the neck area and she started struggling, breathing as though she was losing her life which she later did. Assumpta's father was hit by a big stick on the head which had nails and he collapsed but was still breathing .The militia then got out their machetes and started hacking him as though he was a piece of meat in the butcher. He was hacked several times with a machete and he suddenly lost his life. At that time Assumpta says she fell silent, she didn't fear death at that time and she also wanted to be killed. She was just waiting for the time that she would also die. After the horrific killings of Assumpta's parents the militia left with very happy faces. They continued to the neighborhood and screams were being heard everywhere. Assumpta's uncle then told her that they should continue and run for their lives. As they were running her uncle injured his leg as the militia men were hunting them with dogs. The uncle told her to continue and go and that she should leave him behind. Suddenly Assumpta's friend Jane came running past them very scared and she told Assumpta that the militias were very close. The militias were at Jane's home and they had killed all the family but Jane had escaped and that they were looking for her. Jane told Assumpta that they should run as fast as possible and that they should leave her uncle. Her uncle was then hidden in a nearby bush and the two girls continued their running to safety. That was the last time she saw her uncle alive. They ran their hearts out and they reached a place where they rested for a while. It's from there they started sharing stories of what they had seen and Jane narrated how her mother was killed by hacking her with a machete, her father was then shot, her aunt who was visiting was raped before she was later killed and how they hit the gateman several times with a club on the head and he died on the spot. The two girls then continued running to safety. They ran the whole night and when morning fell there was no one on the streets except the machete welding men. The two girls decided to just hide themselves in nearby swamps. Assumpta says they didn't have any food and the water that was available was full of blood.

In the swamps where they were hiding, there were a lot of people also looking for refuge. The swamps were stinking of blood and corpses were all around. The people who were in the swamps, most of them had injuries and open wounds all over their bodies. For the two days the two girls stayed in the swamps, they had no choice but to drink the blood stained water that was available and also eat the stems of papyrus. As they still hiding in the swamps the girls and other people heard group of men with dogs hunting for people who were hiding in the swamps. They got on their feet, started running as fast as they could and they finally out ran the militia. They decided to leave the swamps and climb up to the hills. They climbed the hill as far as they could go as they wanted to some rest. For the mean time they thought they were safe. The girls heard that the woods were very silent not knowing what was behind the silence. The interhamwe militia had laid an ambush for all the Tutsi survivors who came seeking refuge in the woods but the poor girls didn't know. On realizing that they had fallen into an interhamwe ambush the girls wanted to run but it was impossible as a group of over 10 men had already surrounded them. The soldiers were armed with machetes, guns, clubs and knives. They told the girls to get on their knees which they did. The soldiers started admiring the two girls and they were saying that they had to utilize their beauty since they were going to die anyways. The men then got off their pants as some were holding the two girls down. The girls were then raped in turns by over 10 men up to when they lost consciousness. The girls were screaming but all this was in vain. A man suddenly got out of the blue on hearing the screams with a traditional spear and he was immediately shot by the soldier who was on guard. When Assumpta gained some strength, she got up and asked the militia to just kill her instead of torturing her but the militia just burst into laughter and they instead hacked her with a machete on the head next to the ear and the friend was hacked in the limbs and thereafter left for death. Assumpta was left there helpless and in pain with her dying friend and nothing couldn't do anything neither for her nor herself. The only prayer they prayed was that God could let them rest in peace and let them die quickly. The girls had open infected wounds and they were losing a lot of blood. They spent up to nearly a week in a near death experience without any help coming their way. Suddenly Assumpta remembers seeing something like an angel carrying her and Jane. Fortunately this wasn't an angel and it was the RPF rebels who were taking them to their safe zone. One of the medical soldiers saw the girls and he started crying at the way the girls were handled horrifically. Assumpta and Jane had broken uterus and they were over bleeding. Jane later died on the fourth day in the hospital due to the so many injuries inflicted on her. Assumpta had lost her only friend that she had found and knew. She was taken to Uganda for further medical assistance. Assumpta didn't want to go back to Rwanda after the war but she suddenly changed her mind and went back to Rwanda. She went back to her home and she found it in ruins. When she reached her home, the first thing she did was to clean up the house but she was disturbed by all the memories. She managed to live there for over two months and she was summoned to go and testify in the Gacaca courts. These courts were set up to convict all the people that participated in the killings of innocent Rwandans. After testifying against her neighbors and family friends, she left for home and on her way an old man called her name like he knew her. She looked at the man and it was her only uncle left.

She hugged him tightly and she asked where he was all that time. He replied that he was in a village in Congo. Assumpta was very happy to realize that she at least had a family member to lean on and find the peace and comfort she needed badly. The  happiness didn't last that long as a man came into the house when Assumpta had gone to the market and hacked the uncle to near death and he fell into a comma for 2months. The authorities realized that the man who hacked the uncle was a genocidaire who didn't want to live any witnesses behind. The uncle later survived but lives in constant headaches and mental problems. Assumpta says she tried to commit suicide 2 times after her uncle's incident but she failed. She says she survived the genocide but sometimes she wishes she was dead. She's not able to have children due to the severe damages to her uterus and she's also HIV positive and she says she got the virus from the men who raped her.

Before the genocide she was a young and beautiful girl but today when people tell her she's beautiful, she has no feelings about it and she hates men a lot. She says that sometimes she watches women on the streets happy and wonders why she can't be like them but she remembers she's different and it make her so sad. She says she misses her family and mother a great deal and that she gets nightmares and recalls all the men that raped her and killed her friends and family.

# Sheem's Road To Survival

Sheema is the fifth born in a family of eight siblings. He is now 25years old and remembers that she was about 11 years old when the genocide of 1994 happened. With a family of only eight siblings, only four of them are left to take the tale as the rest of them were killed during the 1994 genocide including both their parents. Sheema says she has been looking after her sibling since 1994.

Sheema explains how she survived with her siblings. Before the genocide her father was a contractor and mother was a housewife. The father took care of the family without any hesitations. They had an average life style like many working class families do. The morning following the announcement of the president's assassination, men armed with guns, machetes, clubs, and grenades overran the whole neighborhood looking for Tutsis families that they were hunting down to kill. The group of militia who also included Sheema's friends and their fathers were seen running around the entire neighborhood singing songs that were enchanting and carried a clear message that they were going to be killed and finished off. Sheema says the genocide had even began earlier through the discrimination that Sheema and her other siblings faced even during their school time. Their teacher who hated them so much was more actively involved in chasing them out of class for no clear reasons and also telling other students to beat them up for no clear reasons. Sheema says that even when they were sent to the markets to buy foodstuffs and other household merchandise they could be denied just for a reason that they were Tutsis and that they didn't deserve anything in the world. Sheema says the leaders in their community could beat up school head teachers could allow Tutsis students to study in their schools. Sheema's classmates even made the lists of people who had to be killed and submitted them to the militia as early as 1993. Sheema says the day the militia came to their home they sensed it quickly and they made a back gate where it would be easy for them to escape. The militias were very annoyed as though Sheema and her family had done something wrong to them.

Sheema says that when they reached the home, they quickly came up and started with killing all their cows. They killed the cows brutally as though they had a problem with them. This clearly meant that the militias were practically ready for anything that would come their way. Sheema and her family that day escaped death because they had a back door they used to escape and this wasn't all, the story had just started. Sheema's father liked to listen to his radio and so he used to carry it wherever he went. On the radio they had announced that roadblocks were set up all over the country. He liked listening to radio Muhabura which the RPF rebels then led by Paul Kagame used to broadcast their message. They then warned the country that they had received intelligence reports that some government officials in the Habyarima government had designed a mass killing master plan for all Tutsis in the country. He then tuned to the RTLM radio which blamed the president's assassination on the Tutsis and the radio was advocating for all Tutsis to take the blame and that they should be killed. As the family escaped from there hideout, they saw a road block manned by the interhamwe militia, and on the road side adjacent to the road block.

Sheema says they saw a lot of people who were Tutsis and some of them were even their neighbours being killed by again there neighbours and the killers seemed to be enjoying what they were doing as they even celebrated with beers and meat that were given by the government officials who ordered them to kill all the innocent people. Sheema says that their parents had wedded a week before in holy matrimony and the people they invited to witness their reunion were the same people who were looking for them wanting to kill them. Sheema's father was really surprised. The road block they saw from a distance had a lot of bodies most of them hacked with machetes. For the second time Sheema and her family had survived death because this was the exact same route they were going to use but she says God saved them from a distance. So they decided to look for another hide out. One of Sheema's sisters saw her friend's home and the friend was a Hutu but she lived alone in the house because she had lost both her parents of natural causes. Sheema's sister went and knocked at the door and the friend opened the door after she explained who she was. The friend then allowed all of them to come and take refuge in the house as outside it was extremely cold. The family was very happy about the decision the friend mad to save them but the happiness didn't even last for that long. On that very night the sister's friend went outside and she told them she was going to buy them food and they were pretty happy about the reception. The young children were put to bed as Sheema's father continued listening to the radio to get all the necessary updates. The events suddenly changed as the friend had gone to invite the militia to her home. Sheema's family didn't detect anything as they thought the girl had no problem and that she was their friend. Sheema's father never knew that woman could also be murderous. At around 8pm that same night the militia invaded the house with Sheema's friend who was also very happy and enjoyed everything. The militia's only mission was to collect money from the family because the friend had told them that the family had a lot of money. A group of 5 men then came up to the family and told them that they were going to kill the whole family if they didn't give them anything. The militias were not even real but rather a mafia group that made a living by stealing from survivors. Sheema's dad then bribed the group leader with a lot of money but he told him that that money was only enough for four people. They were only interested in teasing the family and robbing from them but they didn't have any intentions of killing them. Sheema's dad then directed them to where he had hide the rest of the money and they collected it after which they took him back to his family and told him to disappear with his family that they didn't want to see them that night and for the rest of their remaining days if at all they luckily make it out of the genocide alive. Sheema's mum quickly woke the children who were still sleeping and they went outside running for their lives thinking that the men could change their minds and kill them. Sheema's dad swore never to trust anyone in his life again. They continued on their way to a UN safe camp and by that time they thought they were safe and the UN could protect them from any harm but this wasn't the case either as the UN had been called to withdraw all but most of its troops to go to the airport following the killing of 10 UNAMIR Belgium soldiers. The interhamwe killed each and every person that wanted to escape from the nearby fence to run to the fields.

They had surrounded the whole camp and were just waiting for the UN soldiers to withdraw and they could kill all the innocent civilians. Sheema's dad told the UN soldiers to take them along but they refused saying that they had strict orders not to carry any Rwandans. The UN soldiers were Belgians and this made even the refugees more furious saying to them that they were the ones who started the genocide and that they were the ones that supplied the militia with all the things that they were using to kill them. Sheema's dad called for the soldier to at least kill him first and then his children but they refused and one of them said to them that they should instead protect themselves from the people who were waiting for them outside adding on that he would take them on the truck but they had strict orders not to carry any one on the UN truck and that the trucks were also being searched on the road blocks set up by the army and the militia. The camp was in a missionary school and the soldiers called onto the missionaries to move with them on their trucks but the Reverend fathers and their altar boys refused to board the trucks and said that if they were to take them, they had to also take the people that they were leaving behind. The missionaries knew Sheema's dad as he was the one who helped them construct the school so the father asked the soldiers if they had space for the children, they should at least save the children or else he wasn't going to go anywhere. The UN soldier allowed and so Sheema's dad made Sheema and her sisters climb the truck and he stayed behind. They did all this without realizing that some of the people in the camp were spies. The spies then informed their superiors that there was going to be a truck of UN soldiers that had children of Tutsi origin and that it had to be stopped, take the children off and kill them. Sheema says she and her other siblings were very sad and they cried a lot as they were being driven off to safety leaving their parents behind with the killers. Sheema says it hurts a lot to know that the person you love so much was about to be killed any moment. The UN soldiers hid the children very well that they passed by the militia roadblocks without any hesitation and without them realizing that there were Rwandan nationals also on the trucks. Sheema says that this was the last day she saw her loving parents alive and they too were even crying. The militias were waiting to finish them off as they even called for more militia men to come and carryout the killings saying that the cockroaches were a lot and to finish them all off they needed extra man power. The militia brought in more men to the camp as the trucks were heading outside. The UN soldiers told the children not to bring their heads out at any moment or they would be killed. The trucks moved without any resistance from the roadblocks up to when they reached a roadblock that was being manned by the presidential guard of the Rwandan army then and they ordered everyone out and the UN soldiers refused to move out of the trucks saying that they had strict orders not to stop at any moment. The commander of the UN force ordered his soldiers to prepare for war and that they could shoot anyone who attempted to climb the truck, the presidential guard thought they were a superior force but this time they were outnumbered and so they had no choice but to leave the UN soldiers pass through. Again Sheema and the siblings had escaped death by a whisker but the trials were not yet done. They had gone three days without food and escaped death several times.

The convoy managed to reach hotel mille colline where they had branched off and they had a detache at the hotel and they had to evacuate all the VIPS they said were at the hotel and this was the point where they had to leave the siblings and other children to get space for the VIPS who were saying that they couldn't seat with African children because they were stinking. Sheema says that most of the VIPS were Americans and most of them were investors in Rwanda. The UN army then had to drop off the children at the hotel and they started evacuating their so called VIPS. The siblings were really annoyed but nothing could be done to help them out. After the VIPs were evacuated the UN then left and they left the people at the hotel all alone and no one was able to protect them from open attacks from the militia. On the second day the UN again sent a group of soldiers to come and protect the hotel and all the people that were there were happy again as they couldn't be killed in the presence of the UN. The soldiers were sent to the hotel mainly because the hotel had received some foreign journalists who had come to observe and report what was going on. Some of them while in the field were even assaulted and they often came back with swollen cheeks and though they were beaten up, they never stopped covering the inhuman acts that were taking place all around Kigali and the rest of Rwanda. The siblings were safe for a moment up to when the two younger sisters fell sick and there wasn't any appropriate medicine so one of them died at the hotel and the other was taken to hospital by the hotel management but she was killed when the doctors realized that she was a Tutsi.

There was shortage of water at the hotel and the people at the hotel used to drink the water from the swimming pool and it made some of them sick as it was treated with chemicals. Some of the children literally fell sick but there was no help. The family of 8 was now 6. Sheema says she never slept even a single day without praying for her parents who she thought were dead. Sheema was as healthy as an ox but this didn't last long as she too fell sick and was admitted to a hospital for over six months and by that time the RPF had already captured power but there were a few killings in and out town. Sheema became malnourished because by that time they never even had a single penny to buy food or even take care of their medical bills. They managed to survive up to when the time came for paying the hospital bills and they didn't have any money but one of the soldiers paid for their bills and he even gave them more money for up keep. When the war was done, they decided to return to their real home to see if everything would be okay. But on their way back they met the friend who had sold them to her fellow militia but she ran and they never saw her again up to the time she came at their house at night. The friend who had set them up brought her colleagues to come and finish off the whole family as they thought they could report them to the authorities. They managed to penetrate the house and cut in pieces two of Sheema's siblings who died on the spot. Sheema says they managed to survive all those death trials at the road blocks and also natural causes but only to be killed by such reckless people. Sheema vowed to look for the people who had committed the crimes and that she could take revenge but the government took them for counseling and they got to know why they couldn't carry out the revenge she really wanted. The people who had killed her two siblings were arrested by the authorities and this inspired Sheema to join the army where she still is even up to now.

Sheema says she tried looking for her parents' background but realized that they had been killed and their bodies were dumped in River Nyabarongo. Sheema now takes care of her siblings although she obtained some weird illness when she was still at the hospital. She's now well and vowed to stop genocide in every part of the world at all costs.

# Innocent Ndatimana's Narrow Escape

Innocent was a 38year old Tutsis teacher in the Eastern province of Rwanda in Nyamata sector Bugesera district. Innocent was a history teacher who tried to teach his students the real theories of genocide and used to counsel them about genocide, telling them it was something they did not wish to see in their country because it could be really terrible. Innocent at one time told his students that Rwanda was being driven in the wrong direction by its leaders and that it was the students that had to change the country's fate. He was a well respected man and everyone liked him and they even nick named him teacher of all seasons. When the genocide ideologies started passing through the public, the Hutu community started changing the way they were seeing him and Innocent says he would receive at least a death threat a day.

He says that the genocide ideologies started as way back as 1959 when the first bunch of Tutsis were beaten up, killed and others forced out of the country to the neighboring countries where some of them even got citizenship because they saw no hope of coming back to Rwanda. Innocent's family had been murdered under unclear circumstances and the government soldiers once even arrested him saying he was collaborating with the RPF rebels who wanted to force their way into Rwanda at that time. RPF was a group of young men, most of them sons and daughters of the Tutsis community that escaped the country in 1959 and ran to the neighboring countries of Uganda and Tanzania where they managed to regroup and they wanted to go back to their home country.

The current president of Rwanda then, Juvenal Habyarimana told the rebels who just wanted to come back to their country that Rwanda was like a bottle that is full to the brim and that they had no place in Rwanda. Habyarimana the president of Rwanda had shares in a radio station that was called RTLM which was key in spreading the genocide ideologies. After the president's plane was shot down, the genocide officially started as innocent Tutsis were being killed on the roadblocks that were set up by the government soldiers. Innocent says that he one day survived being killed at the roadblock because he had a student he had taught and was the commander at the roadblock. Innocent says that one thing that hurt him a lot was seeing the students he taught committing the atrocities he had warned them against. Innocent remembers that after that incident he became more cautious on the routes he was using to get in and outside town. He says that his home place Nyamata experienced one of the most brutal killings in Rwanda and this where his students committing the genocide were. He says that students were hacking fellow students and at one time a student also wanted to hack him because he was Tutsi. By the start of April 1994, Innocent was relieved of his duties without giving him a single pay because he was Tutsi. He says that being a Tutsi at that time was a criminal offence that was punished with death. He says that the head teacher of the school he was teaching was swayed into firing Innocent from his job by the parents who were Hutus and they complained that a Tutsis can't teach their children. Innocent says the school never had any history teacher up to when he went back to the chalkboard in 2003.

The district of Bugesera where Innocent lived was a resettlement area for the Tutsis at that time. The leaders in the government at that time wanted to make a place where they could monitor the Tutsis very well. Bugesera was infested with a lot of tsetse flies and mosquitoes and so this was the reason the government sent them there to die slowly. Many people in the area used to die of malaria and other related sickness and the government could nothing. The nearby hospital, the only one in the whole district was in the capital city that was Kigali at that time. And moving there meant going through a lot of roadblocks which clearly meant that Bugesera was an isolation camp.

After the president's plane had been shot down by some mysterious people, the radio that advocated for the genocide was quick to say that it was the Tutsis who did it because they wanted to capture power and that Hutus shouldn't allow the Tutsis reign saying that they should all be killed and that there shouldn't be any trace of them in the whole country. All Tutsis in the country started becoming unsettled from the words that were being said over the radio. Roads blocks manned by the Rwandan army, interhamwe militias and other militias were also erected to provide killing ground for the Tutsis. For a place with a lot of Tutsis families like Bugesera, everyone that wanted to train how they could kill was brought there and a lot of people would be killed as they were being used as training dummies. Innocent still doesn't know how he survived but says it was GOD'S doing to allow him live. On that very night that the plane was brought down, many Tutsis families were killed most especially on the road blocks that were erected most especially by the interhamwe militias group which was a youth political group of the ruling party then the MRND. The interhamwe was designed to support and execute the Hutu ideologies of a republic without the Tutsis in it. The country was no longer safe for the Tutsis and they had to flee but also fleeing was made difficult because of the road blocks erected. Innocent says that the road blocks were also a design to carryout out the genocide. Many Tutsis were arrested and taken to prisons where they could be tortured and later on killed saying that they were collaborators of the RPF rebels yet it wasn't the case. On 11th April 1994, the militia finally came and hit the area and all people were running for their lives as the militias were also shooting aimlessly at running the people.

The communities that were being attacked were unarmed but the people that surely wanted to kill them were heavily armed and they were determined to finish the whole race if they could. Innocent had already lost his family which included his wife and three kids that were murdered by the interhamwe saying that they were Tutsis and so they deserved to die. When things fell apart Innocent didn't have anyone to run with or to save as his whole family was also killed in the 1959 birth of the genocide. The killings started with the assassination of all prominent leaders in the community and also in the country that were Tutsis to silence the voice of this minority ethnic group. When the killings extended from the capital Kigali to the rest of the country and more especially Nyamata, Innocent says he expected it but he didn't believe it would come that soon. The killers didn't spare the children, women nor the elderly. Some of them were only interested in the property of the people they were killing.

As the chaos continued Innocent says the roads leading outside town were cut off and the only refuge was the churches and the town hall where the mayor sat. Innocent says the church was very far so he decided to take refuge in the town hall. While they were in the compound of the hall, the mayor came up and addressed them and told them it wasn't safe at the hall and that he didn't want any bloodshed in the hall and continued to tell them that they were going to be killed anyways. This statement really angered the mob and motivated it to stay at the hall as the mayor was then chased away with stones. But he never gave up, he went ahead and told the interhamwe militia that there were a lot of people that had to be killed hiding at the town hall. After closely an hour, the militia came to prove if it was true and that time they were few so they just passed by and never did anything since they saw that they were outnumbered. Innocent says that the thing that led to many Tutsis losing their lives was that they couldn't defend themselves saying that killings were only for Hutus. And so they could just go down without a fight. Innocent says that youth of about 18years of age could take men of 35years to the slaughter grounds and tell them to kneel down and they could be killed there and then. The militia went back and reorganized. This time they came back with a lot more men and also killing weapons like machetes, clubs, grenades and guns. They came back as determined as never before and they truly wanted to kill and finish off all the people at the town hall. Innocent says everyone that could protect them was nowhere to be seen and the refugees at the hall had heard that people who were seeking refuge at the church had all been killed and finished and this was clearly visible as some of the militias' machetes were filled with blood that was even leaking to the ground.

Innocent says he and other men got stones and they started throwing them at the advancing determined militia but they weren't moved as they kept on advancing and they then threw a grenade right next to where Innocent and other men were standing and he unfortunately lost a leg. Then the militia came up to them with much hate and hacked all but most of the men that were shooting the stones. The militia then reached where Innocent was and they hacked him several times in the limbs and they continued to the town hall where they were throwing grenades at the mob and also killing the other people by hitting them with clubs that had nails at their ends and that's where many people perished. Innocent says up to now he doesn't know how he found himself in the RPF camp.

He says that from all the people who were at the hall, who were about 25,000, not more than 30 people survived. This is the place where more people were brutally killed, and the militia didn't even spare the men and women. Innocent says that some people were even thrown in the latrines and others taken to mass graves alive. Innocent says that he survived by God's grace and that's why he gave his remaining part of his life to serving the Lord and also his people. He says when he survived he lived in Uganda for three years but he saw no progress in his life and so he had to move back to his original home in Rwanda. He lost a leg but he isn't hurt as he knows that at least he still has his life and his head is still working and still teaching his new era of students. The region of Eastern province was the most hit since it was believed that most Tutsis were living there. Luckily it was the first to be recovered by the RPF rebels but the moment they recovered the area an uncountable number of people had lost their lives.

He is a history teacher now and teaches his students while showing them the injuries he sustained through the genocide. He says the only torment he faces is that of seeing the people who tried to kill him still moving on the streets but his family is nowhere to be found. When he returned to Rwanda he went ahead and got another wife and they are happily married with 2 children and he hopes he can change the way they think through teaching them the good and bad. This wasn't taught to the people who managed to take away someone's life. He now gives testimonies about the genocide and says that this should never happen anywhere in the world.

# Valentina 2 fled to the church

It all began on a Friday afternoon in the middle of April. For days the Tutsis of Nyarubuye had sensed an impending disaster. They were aware that elsewhere in the country massacres of Tutsis had already begun. Ten days prior to that, Juvenal Habyarimana, the president of Rwanda, had been assassinated, most probably by members of his political circle. Although he was a Hutu, Habyarimana was seen as having become weak in his dealings with the Tutsis and the moderate Hutus' opposition groups. The extremists feared that the power-sharing agreement signed by Habyarimana would see the erosion of their power and financial privilege. His death which was caused by a plane crash, the extremists blamed on the Tutsis and this provided the pretext for a "final solution" in which all Tutsis and Hutu moderates were to be killed. It would result in the murder of all Tutsis across the country as they were now considered to be "*dirty cockroaches*" that were unworthy of living.

As a result, the killings were launched and Tutsis whether old or young started dying in massive numbers. The women were considered as the spoils of the genocide and most of them were being raped, mutilated and later on killed. The few ones that managed to survive were forcefully taken as wives or slaves.

The killings at Nyarubuye began with an attack on Tutsis at the local marketplace. After this incident, Valentina fled to the church with her family hoping to find there refugee and protection from the killers who were determined to finish them off at all costs. Valentina was the last born in her family that only comprised of her mother who was a nursery school teacher in Nyarubuye, her father who was a mechanic and her who had joined secondary shortly before the genocide started. They were a happy family, moderately rich and were also good Christians. They were peaceful people and it was very hard to hear that Mr. Hakizimaana, Valentina's father was involved in a conflict whether at the work place, or in the neighborhood. To them, the word violence never existed in their vocabulary. Valentina speaks of her mother as a very beautiful woman not only on the outside but also the inside. She recalls that every Sunday evening, her mother would gather all the children in the neighborhood and would give them cake as she loved to bake. "It was her hobby," says Valentina. She adds on that she was named after her mother and always dreamt of being just like her when she grows up. For Valentina, the death of her parents is a wound that will never heal and she hopes that one day she will be reunited with them in heaven. She didn't know much about her elder brother Frodise only that he was very stubborn, loved soccer and was very protective of her.

On the day that marked the beginning of the killings in Nyarubuye, Valentina says that it was chaos and flames everywhere. People were being killed all around the area and the only safe place at that moment was the local church where they always attended Sunday mass. However that wasn't possible as the church was also attacked. That afternoon the killers arrived, led by Sylvestre Gacumbitsi, the local mayor. The reverend father couldn't save anyone as he was the first one to be shot dead when he got in the killers' way trying as much as he could to save his people. Valentina recognized many of her Hutu neighbors among the more than 30 men who surrounded the church. They carried knives, machetes, grenades and clubs that had nails at their ends and were supported by soldiers from the Rwandan army. Among the gang of men was Denis Bagaruka, grandfather whose own grandchildren lived and played with Valentina. This old man was their neighbor and one time Valentina's mother had looked after him at the hospital while he was sick. She described what happened next:

"First they asked people to hand over their money, saying they would spare those who paid. But after taking the money they killed them anyway. Then they started to throw grenades. I saw a man blown up in the air, in pieces, by a grenade. The leader said that we were snakes and that to kill snakes you had to smash their heads. The killers moved into the terrified crowd of men, women and children, hacking and clubbing as they went. The pregnant women among the crowds were taken out and their unborn babies cut out as they looked on but after a very short while, they would also die due to over bleeding and extreme pain. If they found someone alive they would smash their heads with stones. I saw them take little children and smash their heads together until they were dead. Some were thrown against the walls like the babies and their heads would burst into pieces. There were children begging for pity but they killed them straight away," she told. The killings took place over for four days. At night the butchers rested and guarded the perimeter so that nobody would escape. They would also take out young girls aged between 14 and 18 and would repeatedly rape them in gangs. Those who tried to resist would be mutilated and left there to bleed to death. Other infants, crying on the ground beside their murdered parents, were taken and plunged head first into latrines. One of Valentina's classmates, and angel-faced little boy named Placide, <u>told me</u> how he had seen a man decapitated in front of him and then a pregnant woman cut open as the killing reached its frenzied climax. "There was so much noise," he recalled. People were begging for mercy and you could hear the militia saying, "Catch them, catch them and don't let them get away." Valentina and Placide hid among the bodies, pretending to be dead as it was the only way to survive being killed. Valentina had been struck on the head and hands with a machete and was bleeding heavily. Following her child's instinct, she crawled to her mother's body and lay there. During the killing she had seen the militia murder her father and her 16-year-old brother, Frodise then later on her mother. Valentina was now all alone with no one to cry too for help and surrounded by death in every corner. Her life was already going slowly by slowly because of the heavy wounds she carried both on her body and in her heart. After several days Valentina crawled to the room where there were fewest bodies. For the next 43 days she lived among the rotting corpses, too weak to stand up and convinced that the world had come to an end and no one would come to her rescue. By then the killers had moved on searching and wiping out Tutsis. They attacked a primary school that was next to the church and over 100 people that were hiding there were killed. Some were struck with machetes while others were tied up in groups and bombed to death. Valentina says that on one time, the killers returned to the school, locked up all the remaining people who were mostly children and burnt them alive. Some were even her schoolmates and friends. She went ahead and added that she had painful screams shouting out for mercy but all in vain as the killers were jubilating cursing them that they were never supposed to have been born and that they deserved to be burnt to death just like rubbish. *"I prayed that I would die because I could not see a future life ahead of me. I did not think that anybody was left alive in the country. I thought everybody had been swept away"*, she said.

She drank rainwater and rummaged for scraps of food. There was some wild fruit and some grain but she became weaker and weaker as the days progressed. Her wounds were infected and had even started to rot. In the weeks that followed, a few other children emerged from hiding places around the church. Some were heavily wounded like Valentina and others even worse. She recalls seeing some of them die because of pain in their wounds and hunger. This made Valentina feel more scared as she knew that very soon she too was going to die just like the others. Some of them wandered off hoping to find a better place but were eventually killed as they were roadblocks manned by the intarahamwe at every corner. The remaining ones became Valentina's new family at the moment. The stronger ones lit fires and cooked what food they could find, feeding the weaker ones like Valentina. At night, she says they would all gather themselves around and pray for their loved ones who had been killed already. They would ask God to continue keeping them alive and spare them from the blades of the intarehamwe. From the dead bodies around them, they would take clothes from them to cover themselves up from the cold most especially the injured ones. Valentina says that the stronger boys would risk their lives in the mornings and go out to hunt for food and water. She recalls that on one Sunday morning, as usual the boys went out to look for food but on their way back they fell into an ambush and as they ran away escaping from the militias two of them were shot dead. This weakened Valentina and the others more as their strongest saviors were no longer there to fend for them. For the following days, they went without food or water which weakened them more. Most of them started dying one by one most especially the little ones and the wounded. But despite it all Valentina managed to still push through. She managed to find some cleaner clothes from a dead baby's body and covered on her wounds. During the nights, they would hear explosions and people crying out for help. They couldn't sleep as they carried on in the night on tension and fear that the killers would come back for them. The stench of the dead bodies was also mounting up but Valentina and her friends had nothing to do but to put up with it as the only safe hide out was among the smelly corpses.

Then a new hazard appeared: wild dogs that had started to eat the corpses. "The dogs were coming at night and eating dead children in the other rooms. A dog came to where I was and started to eat a body. I picked up a stone and threw it at the dog and drove it away." At a certain point dogs would invade them at night and try to eat them as they were no more corpses to eat. They onetime ate a young girl who was so weak to defend herself from them and even her friends couldn't save her as the dogs were too fierce. With time the situation worsened and they had to vacate the place or else be eaten by the dogs. They decided to go the nearby convent that belonged to the church. There they were a lot of survivors hiding in the chapel and others outside in the compound. The nuns weren't that receptive and always kept threatening the people that they were to be killed and had to leave the chapel saying that they didn't want wreckage in their convent. The nun who kept threatening them more was the Mother superior known as Sister Benedicte Mukanyangezi. She was Hutu. She was a fat and short, wore big glasses and always put on a wicked smile. She wasn't compassionate at all. This Sister even reached a point where she locked the gates of the convent refusing people to come in and looked on as they were being killed just at the entrance of the convent. For three days, Valentina, her friends and the other people continued to hide at the convent despite the continuous threats from Sister Benedicte. With the help of two sisters, Valentina was able to receive some medical care and they were also given food, water and clean clothes. These two Sisters were Tutsis. On the fourth day of their stay, Sister Benedicte came into the chapel and tried to force the people out saying that she could no longer keep them at the convent knowing exactly that once they go out on the streets they would all be killed. Despite the plea of the mothers and young children Valentina inclusive, she refused and even tried to use force to throw them out. With such treatment, the men fought back and continued to force their stay in the convent. For the next two days the Sister never returned and they all thought that she had gave up on throwing them out not knowing that she was in meetings with the intarahamwe planning their death.

Valentina recalls that it was on a Sunday morning after mass when Sister Benedicte sent most of the nuns who were against her evil doings to go and help out at the health center saying that the work load over there was over whelming and the superintendent needed extra help. However this was among the plan to get them out of her way such that she and the intarahamwe could finish of the Tutsis at the convent. Once the other nuns left, her together with her assistant known as Sister Josephine came into the convent with about five armed men and ordered all the people to step outside. Those who tried resisting were instantly shot dead. This was a sign of warning to the rest. Upon seeing that, they all peacefully step out and lined up according to their sex. Valentina and her friends were put among the rest of the other children. They were then told to walk towards the convent fields were they were to be massacred from. They started with the men first and most of them were struck on neck. They even went ahead and ordered some of them to kill their fellow Tutsis promising them to be spared from death but after they too were killed. When they had finished killing most of them, they went to the women. Most of them were brutally raped at first then killed. The young pretty ones were spared to become their concubines. It was awful according to the way most of these women were killed. Valentina says that some were pierced with long sharp sticks in their vaginas and tear them apart while others would be heavily clubbed in their private parts until they would die. Valentina says that she reached a point when she could no longer cry but just look on. To her it was like a long nightmare she couldn't escape from. When their time came, she and the rest were locked up in a store and it was set on fire. At that point Valentina had lost her mind and for over half an hour she watched some of her fellow children chock to death while others were already burning. With this, the killers started leaving with the girls and women they had held captive. Valentina was able to escape with two other boys with the help of the two Tutsi nuns who had stayed back doing their daily chores. However when Sister Benedicte learnt about that they had helped Tutsi children escape, she ordered for their death and they too were murdered. Valentina suffered severe burns on her right leg and couldn't run any further. The other two boys later managed to take to the health center where they too hid. At that moment, Valentina passed herself off as a Hutu as she was dark skinned and a bit short. The nurses there treated her burns and for a whole week she managed to get some rest. This too didn't last that long as the intarahamwe invaded the health center saying that there were Tutsi children hiding among the patients. Valentina knew that she would be recognized by them as the two leaders were from her neighborhood.

With no other alternative, she and the two boys took and left the health center from the back doors but they didn't go that far. They hid inside the broken ambulance that was parked at the back of the health center. It's from there Valentina watched how the rest of the other children and patients were put to death. Most of the babies and toddlers were killed by the nurses themselves. For Valentina, death had become a common sight before her eyes. When it started getting back, she and the two boys one named Paulo crawled out and embarked on a journey that led them to the Rwanda Congo boarder. On their way they would pass by dead bodies, some even rotten with bones only remaining. The streets smelled. Dogs and vultures came from every corner to fed on the dead flesh of people. It was very disgusting and at one point Valentina vomited because of the awful stench that covered the streets. Since roadblocks were everywhere, they decided to go off road and moved in the bushes and swamps. It was very hard for Valentina to move with a wounded leg but she had to gather all strength or else die at the hands of the intarahamwe. While in the bushes and swamps, they came across other surviving Tutsi some also wounded. It's from there that these children came across a young man who managed to help them reach and cross the border as the distance was long and couldn't manage anyways. For a few days, they stayed with him in the bush but as the killings intensified, the bushes also became unsafe and they had to vacate them. Valentina was now too weak and couldn't walk anymore so the man carried her on his back while Paulo and the other boy followed. They managed to come across a red cross truck that was heading to Congo and when the driver so the children and the poor state Valentina was in, he felt pity for them and decided to hide them in the truck. He managed to drive them up to the boarder but the young man was discovered by the militia and his journey to safety ended there as he was killed. Luckily for Valentina and the boys, the passed through and camped at a refugee camp in Goma. Valentina was able to get her wounds treated but since her burnt leg had stayed without treatment for so long, it was badly infected and had to be cut off so as to save her life. The other boy too died just after two days when they had arrived at the health center. According to Valentina, he had eaten some poisonous wild fruits while they hid in the bushes. She stayed with Paulo who tried his best to comfort her and try to make her believe that things will get better even if she has one leg. It was very hard for Valentina to accept the fact that she was lame and would never be normal like the rest. She even tried to take her own life by drowning herself in a pond but was quickly rescued. Valentina's mental condition worsened and was transferred to a mental hospital in Kinsasha. She says that life there was very hard and at one point, she raped by one of the male nurses who were supposed to look after her. This made her sink further into depression asking herself why life was so cruel towards her. This nurse not only raped her once nut several times until one day one female doctor caught him in the act. Valentina says that he would come into her room, inject with things that would always weaken her to a point where she couldn't even cry out for help but just moan as tears ran down her eyes. When she was finally saved from this torture by this female doctor, Valentina begged her to take her with her promising to do anything. The doctor agreed but when they arrived home, she only treated Valentina well for a few days and later on turned her into a maid. As the discussion went on, Valentina told me that she used to work like a horse from morning until late in the night when the doctor would come back from drinking. She said that there were nights she could get so drunk and return and beat Valentina up to a point of fainting. This went on until Valentina couldn't bear it anymore. The doctor had even started making plans to start selling her off to men but Valentina managed to escape in time before she put her plans into action. For weeks, Valentina managed to trace her way back to the camp where she was able to find Paulo, the boy she had escaped with from Rwanda. At first he couldn't even recognize her as she was all wasted and her clothes were all rugs. But when he looked at her walking stick, he remembered as he was the one that had adjusted it and made it a little bit more comfortable for Valentina. They reunited and days after they managed to board the bus that was returning the Rwandese refugees back to their homes.

When Valentina arrived back in Rwanda, it was around at the end of 1995. She went back to her home hoping she would at least find someone among those they had left behind but they were all murdered. Even the house was in ruining. Their whole property had been stolen and the few that remained were destroyed. For her friend Paulo he had nowhere and no one to turn too as his whole family starting from the grandparents was all killed. So for the first few weeks, Valentina and Paulo managed to stay at an old woman's home who later helped Valentina trace her remaining relatives which was her aunt. This old woman was once her babysitter while she was still a little baby.

There comes a point in the telling of this story where the existing vocabulary of suffering becomes inadequate, where words wither in the face of an unrelenting darkness. As a reporter I found this the most difficult story of my career to tell. As a parent I listened to Valentina's story with a sense of heartbreak. I marveled at her courage but felt deep anger that this shouldn't happen to any child. It was difficult to keep those feelings in check when I confronted one of the butchers of Nyarubuye in the office of the local prosecutor.

Bagaruka, the grandfather who witnesses say was an enthusiastic killer, had recently returned from Tanzania. He had spent nearly three years there in the refugee camp at Benaco where he and his family were fed and cared for by the international community. The man who had helped to bring terror to the infants of Nyarubuye was nervous and evasive when I spoke to him.

"You have eight children, how in God's name can you help to kill a child?" I asked him. After a long pause he answered: "You see all those people in the church had children. Many were carrying them on their backs but none survived. Everyone was killed. We couldn't spare the children's lives. Our orders were to kill everyone. If you did otherwise to what was ordered, you would also be killed. He told me that he himself had been an orphan and a Tutsi man had been his guardian. Bagaruka had seen the man killed at Nyarubuye. *"I almost become crazy when I think about that,"* he said as he couldn't risk his life to save him.

Bagaruka has confessed to some of his crimes and has implicated some of his friends and neighbours, hoping to save himself from the firing squad.

Valentina hopes he will never return to the village. She now lives with an aunt and two other orphans. The aunt's husband and three children were killed at Nyarubuye. Valentina says that with the help of some good Samaritans who came to the village, she was able to get a plastic leg and now move around freely. She and Paulo whose one of the two orphans staying with her aunt were able to go back to school and are on government scholarships. She told me that although she's living a better life, she is not completely happy as every night she dreams of her parents being killed and children burning. She at times wakes up in the middle of the night screaming for help. This has negatively affected her in her studies although her aunt has tried her best to help her forget those traumatizing memories through taking her to counseling sessions. Valentina's aunt also managed to get hold of Valentina's parents remains and bury them decently. Valentina seeks refuge in writing and she hopes that one she will write a book about her tragedy life and that of her fellow children.

## Jason Nshimye

Every year in Rwanda, celebrations are held countrywide in remembrance of all the innocent lives of men, women and children that perished in the 1994 genocide. The genocide started in April 1994 after the crash of president Juvenile Habyarimana's plane something that was blamed on the Tutsis saying that they had planned his death so as to take over the power that according to the Hutus, it belonged to them. Although Tutsis were being murdered even far back from the 1959s, it was done silently not until April 1994 after the death of the president. News spread across the country mobilizing Hutus to eliminate all Tutsis and moderate Hutus. According to the Hutus, the Tustsis were a cursed race and had no right to live in Rwanda. They were regarded as cockroaches that were finishing up Rwanda and for that reason they had to be wiped out. It didn't long when the killings started beginning from the capital city Kigali. The killers who were known as Intarahamwe started with killing all the Tutsis who were in the government by then. The first person was their very own Prime Minister Agatha Uwilingyimana who was murdered on 7th April 1994. She had served the Rwandan government from 18th July 1993 to the day she was killed. Most of her colleagues were also killed apart from a few that managed to escape with their families. After killing most of the Tutsis who served in the government and some Hutu moderates who were against the genocide ideology, the killings were turned to the civilians majority Tutsi and a few Hutus who collaborated with them.

Jason Nshimye now aged 36 lived to tell the story. He says that the events of April 1994 will always stay fresh in his memory. He was 15 years a high school sophomore by the time the genocide started. To him it's like yesterday and that despite all the efforts and counseling, he hasn't managed to forget. He says he forgave those who hurt him but can't erase what they did to him. Nshimye was the first born among four in his family and he's the only one that survived the genocide. They lived in Mugonero. His father was a doctor at the government hospital in Mugonero while the mother operated a retail shop in the main Mugonero market. His three sisters all attended the Mugonero government primary school. They were a happy family that never lacked anything and lived in peace and harmony. Nshimye was even among the football team at his school and held the position of defender. Nshimye says he was doing very well in school not only in sports but also in academics. Some of his classmates envied him. Apart from being bright and talented, Nshimye was very handsome. The girls used to describe him as the *"School Romeo"*. He was a very popular student all around the school campus. He says that had it all life could offer. A loving supporting family, a nice school and also a career in the making. He wanted to be a football star and play for one of the best teams in Europe. However all his dreams were swept away the day the intarahamwe invaded their village killing every Tutsi they came across. Houses were burning, children screaming and women yelling for help. It was chaotic. Nshimye and his three sisters were having lunch when this broke out. So frighten and scared, they locked themselves in the house and managed to stay there until the evening when their father managed to trace his way back home with the mother. On reaching home, he said that it was dangerous every where most especially in the town square as the first roadblock in Mugonero was manned there. That night, they never got any sleep as they spent the whole of it packing and hiding some of their most valuable belongings. His father had managed to collect a lot of money saying that it was to be used to bribe the Intarahamwe and also find them transport to the boarder leading to Congo as he had some good friends there. These were mostly his classmates he studied with medicine. In the morning as they got ready to leave, a young man who worked as a janitor at the hospital where Nshimye's father worked came and informed them that it was very deadly to use the main roads as roadblocks had been manned up everywhere most especially at the exit points. With that warning, Nshimye and his family took short cuts but they hardly made it any far as gunshots were in every corner. They therefore decided to hide at the church where two of his sisters were choir members. At the church, they found there many other Tutsi who had also come to seek refuge. Some were even already wounded with gunshots. Nshimye said that when they had just settled down, a heavily pregnant woman came in badly wounded and  gave birth to a baby girl but died just after it was born leaving the little infant with behind. He remembers seeing some of the women who were at church get hold of the child and took it with them but it was very difficult for it to have lived for long as it was very weak and could hardly even make a sound. For a few days they managed to hide in the church without any problems until they started getting threats from the pastor himself.

According to him, they were dirtying his church and putting his property at risk. But it was expected as he was Hutu. At that moment he had forgotten that the people he was throwing out were once his devoted Christians. Some of them even his choir members like Nshimye's two sisters. This was when he realized that even a church could be a killing field. He thought no one would kill anyone in a church, they started hearing rumors that people were already being killed in the churches they had went too hoping to be safe, so him and the family decided to run away but failed as they had nowhere to escape too at that moment. Nshimye then overheard people saying that they were next, that the next day, they would all be killed. A group of Tutsi leaders wrote to the president of the church, pleading for his help.

*"Our dear leader, Pastor Elizaphan Ntakirutimana,"* their letter began. It then urged the pastor to speak with the mayor to appeal

for his guests' lives. *"We believe that, with the help of God, who entrusted you the leadership of this flock, which is going to be destroyed, your intervention will be highly appreciated, the same way as the Jews were saved by Ester. We give honor to you."* That appeal fell on deaf ears. *"He was Hutu. He was one of the criminals,"* explained Nshimye. *"He told us, no matter what we tried to do, we would be killed anyway."*

Death arrived the next morning. "The Hutu killers came from every direction and surrounded the church. They had hand grenades, guns, clubs and machetes," said Nshimye. People were dying in every corner and everywhere I looked, hundreds, every minute. He witnessed many of his family members and closest friends die that day. His father was shot in the head and he install died. The mother and his three sisters were all raped in the pastor's house. Nshimye says, "with his own eyes, he saw the pastor forcing himself on his mother. He couldn't do anything to help her nor the sisters. They were then tied up and burnt alive under a mango tree where they used to make choir practices from. Nshimye managed to escape, running into the bushes. *"I hid there for weeks,"* he said. *"But every day the Hutus came to hunt and kill."* In the rough, Nshimye met 8-year-old Françoise, the girl who would later become his wife. *"When I met her, she'd lost her whole family too. "For three months, they hid together, constantly on the run, unable to go to a grocery store or hospital. Nowhere was safe. "Even the wounded victims who survived their attempted killers,"* explained Nshimye, *"were betrayed and finished off by the doctors and nurses meant to save them."* It was death everywhere. While in the bushes, people would come in badly wounded. Some even died from there with no one to help them. In the mornings, hunting dogs would raid the bushes looking for Tutsis. Nshimye says at one point he had to put his fright aside and kill one of those dogs or else he and Francoise die at their mercy.

They were trained dogs and would bite their victims to death then after feed on them.

In less than 100 days, more than 800,000 Rwandans were killed. The world stood by as Rwanda tore itself apart. *"There was nowhere to run to,"* remembers Nshimye. *"There were military roadblocks and trained Hutu civilian checkpoints everywhere."* The Tutsis were being systematically eliminated. *"One day they almost caught me,"* he remembers. He was walking with a group of children when a member of the military stopped them. *"The guy had a gun. But I thought we would be OK. I had small kids with me."* Then Nshimye heard these words: *"Lie down and I'll kill you,"* the soldier said. He fired, shooting each of the children dead before Nshimye's eyes. Nshimye knew he was next. *"He pointed the gun at my head. He shot. But, there were no bullets left. It was a miracle. I survived."* He ran as fast as his legs could take him to find Francoise where he had hid her. Luckily she was alright. So they moved to an abandoned house and hid in the wreckages. Those were to be their new house for the days that followed. Nshimye would go out during the day to look for food and water. At times he would manage to get but there are times he failed and would sleep on empty stomachs. There wasn't much to eat. There's even a time they spent almost a week with nothing to eat. Day and night, they hid there as it was extremely dangerous to go out on the streets. The fighting had intensified. One the eighth day, Nshimye managed to sneak out and see if he could find something for the little girl. She was becoming weaker and weaker. While out on the hunt for food, he overheard that in the neighboring village the RPF had over taken and were now guarding it. This was good news but how to get there was a serious problem. They were roadblocks everywhere and the militias were on watch 24/7 to make sure no one escapes alive. Back in the wreckage house Francoise was very weak and she could hardly stand on her feet. Nshimye had to think of a plan to save both his and her life. She was all <u>he had and had</u> grown very fond of her. For about three days he watched the killers' movements, when they were active and when they rested. In the evenings, the killers would gather around fires and celebrate the day's killing while they share what they have looted. At times some would disagree and end up fighting. The women and young girls they held captive, they would take them out and rape them in groups from there. Every night there would be screams of people pleading for help and mercy. After days of good observation, Nshimye together with Francoise decide to move and relocate to the safe zone that was under the guard and control of the RPF. The RPF was also a military group of Tutsi and Hutu moderates who had left Rwanda during the 1959s and had returned to liberate Rwanda from the extremist rule of the Hutus. This liberation force was led by Paul Kagame who is now the current president of Rwanda. The escape wasn't easy especially for Nshimye as he had to hold Francoise on his back since she couldn't walk. As the roads were very risky, they passed in the swamps because they were the only place that was bit safe. He said that in the swamps too, many dead bodies some even rotten were all scattered. On top of that, the swamps had snakes which also made it impossible for them to get around quickly. He said that those who had managed to survive being killed by the intarahamwe and hid in the swamps, they were bitten by snakes and many of them died as they couldn't get medical treatment. Nshimye and Francoise stayed in the swamps for over five days. He says it was God's grace that they managed to stay alive and not bitten by the snakes. For those days they drunk from the swamp and ate papyrus stems. Although very dirty stained with blood, it was the only water available. Little by little they drew closer to the safe zone but Nshimye says he doesn't remember how they got there. He only recalls waking up in a white room that looked like a hospital. It was a hospital. They informed him that they had been found by the RPF who were doing patrol on the boarders of the safe zone. Nshimye had fainted because of the long journey and extreme hunger. For Francoise although she was still alive, she was very malnourished and was being admitted in intensive care unit.

Not only did he survive, but he stayed in Rwanda to help others. After the killings stopped, he went on to graduate from nursing school and quickly returned to his home village to help both survivors and those suspected in the murders. With the help from the new government and support from some health organization like the Red Cross, Nshimye and the rest of the other volunteer doctors managed to treat many survivors. He says that it felt good extending a helping hand to the helpless people most especially children. They also constructed orphanages for the young ones that had lost their parents. Nshimye says that at first the living conditions were that good but with time he managed to adjust as it was much better than during the fighting. Counseling centers were also set up and they helped Nshimye and his fellow survivors open up and talked about what was done to them. This made him realize that he wasn't the only emotionally suffering. They also helped them forgive the people who had brought so much injury in their lives. *"This reconciliation,"* says Nshimye, *"helped me to heal my psychological and spiritual wounds."*

Two decades have passed since the Rwandan genocide. But Nshimye's memories haven't faded. He doesn't want them to. *"Even speaking about it today,"* he says, *"it's hard to explain the tragedy. It was horrible."* Rather than forget, he chooses to forgive. He credits his unwavering faith. *"During this time,"* he says, *"I was terrified and horrified, but I kept my hope in the everlasting God. He looked down upon me or else I wouldn't have lived until now."*

Today Nshimye lives in Richmond, Va., with Françoise and their three children. "*Now I have a happy life*," he says simply. "*My children attend school, I have a good job that enables me look after my loved ones*." He adds on. And as he sees it, Rwanda has a bright future. A few years ago, he returned home and to the church that became a grave site for so many of his loved ones. "*Everything was different*," he said. "We don't have people asking: "*Are you Hutu or Tutsi?*" People are living together as one". The economy of Rwanda is growing. People are working harder now. People are going to school. The country is building a foundation for a peaceful future and a peace. Those who accepted their crimes served their sentences and now live freely among them. Nshimye says that he even treats them when they come to the hospital where he works.

# ACRONYMS AND EXPLANATORY NOTES

*Inkotanyi*, was used to refer to the RPF by both its allies and opponents. The terms, which means "fierce fighters" in Kinyarwanda, was the name given to one of the battalions of King Rwabugiri in the nineteenth century.

*Inyenzi*, meaning "cockroach" in Kinyarwanda, was a term of abuse for the RPF made popular by the Habyarimana. The term has another connation; after the massacres and expulsions of Tutsi in 1959-63, a group of refugees, called Inyenzi, tried to stage a comeback and were defeated. The term was intended to imply that the RPF had the same objectives, and was equally destined to fail.

RPF: Rwandese Patriotic Army

MRND: National Revolutionary Movement for Development

UNAMIR: United Nations Assistance Mission to Rwanda

AVEGA: Association of the Widows of the Genocide of April 1994

# HAMID BAROLE ABDU

Hamid Barole Abdu was born in Asmara, Eritrea, in 1953. He has been living in Italy since 1974 and throughout his career he has shown great interest in different forms of arts including prose, poetry and theatre. Among his publications:

**1986-** *"Eritrea a culture to be saved"*; A brochure about the history, culture and traditions of Eritrea.

**1996-** *"Akhria, I uprooted poet through hunger."* This second publication won, in 1996, the XIII edition of the literary prize "Satyagraha" of Riccione.

**2001-** *"Dreams and nightmares of an undocumented immigrant."* This collection of poems is closely related to the immigrant experience and thereby explores the themes of nostalgia and displacement.

**2005-** *"How not to be mistaken for a cigarette lighter hawker at the beach."* The article has been published both in the anthology *"Migrantemente- il popolo invisibile prende la parola"* and in the collection of poems and short stories "Bury my skin in Africa". Written with a pinch of humor, this short story provides specific suggestions for dark skinned people who intend to take a relaxing beach holiday.

**2006-** *"Bury my skin in Africa"*, a collection of poems and short stories which won in 2007 the prize Multietnicità e Intercultura. Edited by Artestampa, the book has been  translated into Italian and English. The idea of this publication arises from a trip made by the author at the end of 2004 in Sudan, along the border with Eritrea. During this trip, the author visited several refugee camps where Eritrean people live under miserable life conditions and on his own initiative, he decided to devote the proceeds of the book's sales to school-age Eritrean children. All funds raised have been used to purchase didactic materials and give them the opportunity to have access to education.

**2009-** "***Green monkeys***." Written with the journalist Daniele Barbieri, this performance for theatre has been presented in more than 100 italian cities. The text is written in the form of a monologue and it's based upon a conversation between an italian and an immigrant. Moreover, it has been published in the anthology "***Limite acque scure***", a collection of stories edited in 2009 by Massimo Avenali (Noubs editions). In the same year and in occasion of the World aids day, Hamid Barole and Daniele Barbieri presented the monologue "Conversando con un virus".

**2010-** "***Mohammed's fly***" is an anthology of selected poems edited by Libertà Edizioni. The homonym poem "Mohammed's fly" has been selected for different poetry festivals and competitions and turned into a short film. It may be seen by clicking:

https://www.youtube.com/watch?v=yBHhrbMctRo

In the same year he contributed with some poems to the collection "***Permit of Stay in Italy***", an anthology of short stories by various foreign writers edited by Angelo Ferrucci, Ediesse Publishing (2010).

**2013-** "***Verses of renewal and ... Wandering ... hope***." This collection of poems reflects once again the involvement of the author towards the conditions of immigrants. These conditions are translated into fragments of life and death which inevitably overlap each other. In 2013 he published as well some poems for the collection "***100 thousand poets for change***" (Qudulibri)

**2014-** In 2014 Hamid Barole wrote some poems for the collection "***Under the sky of Lampedusa – Drowned from refoulement***", with a preface by Erri De Luca, Publishing by Rayuela (2014).

In addition to the publications, the author regularly contributes to online magazines and websites. He also conducts intercultural workshops with students attending middle and high school. There are also some projects in progress including: "***B.O.H., What the new president of the United States  will do***", "***Omsizzar-  The role of  the media with regard migration***" and "***The black memory***" a performance that retraces the history of Africa from the slave trade period to the globalization era. As to the full length film "***Il vicario del Diavolo***", it tells the story of an egyptian boy and his involvement in international terrorism.

"***Poems through the pearl of Africa***", is a collection of poems written by students of literature of Makerere College School which is located in Kampala, Uganda. Edited by Hamid Barole Abdu and translated in Italian by Daniela Buccioni. The book will be published soon in a bilingual Italian-English.

"***Childhood in War, Blood and Violence***"

"**Genocide in Rwanda -** *Testimonies of Survivors*"

For further details on how to arrange a presentation, if you have any questions about the book or you want to buy it, please contact us through the following channels:

www.hamidbarole.it

http://www.facebook.com/baroleabdu

E-mail: hamidbarole@libero.it

Italy:　　　　+339.5919387

Uganda:　　　+256(0)783265136

**Genocide in Rwanda - *Testimonies of Survivors,*** it is true time heals all wounds and the pain felt today will be less than what the heart will feel tomorrow. But then history cannot be erased. And the Rwanda genocide left wounds that may hurt less now but whose scars remain so visible. Recorded herein are life changing stories of some genocide survivors. Only they can best describe their fears, struggles and turmoil.

A period of 3 months saw members of the Hutu ethnic majority murder as many as 800,000 people, mostly of the Tutsi minority. Ordinary citizens were incited by local officials and the Hutu-led government to take up arms against their neighbours, friends, in-laws and wives. Hutus of all ages were trained to be strong, brutal and vigilant while conducting acts of hatred against the Tutsis.

Countless children watched as their parents were killed. Men were forced to cut off their wives' heads. Mothers helplessly looked on as their babies were burnt. Only a few narrowly escaped the catastrophes that happened so fast leaving the entire country in a desperate state.

By the time the Tutsi-led Rwandese Patriotic Front gained control of the country, hundreds of thousands of Rwandans were dead not only from the massacres but also from hunger and disease. Many more had been displaced from their homes while others still live with the guilt participating in the murders. Today, they have enough courage to share their experiences.

https://www.youtube.com/watch?v=jub7gco054g